POSTPARTUM

The Expectations & Reality of the Fourth Trimester

J. DAWSON

Printed in the United States of America

First Printing, 2023

ISBN: 979-8-218-28761-0

HMD Publications
Denver, Colorado

DEDICATION

This book is dedicated to my daughter Harper. Without her, I never would have known the depth of love I am capable of nor the amount of strength within my body and mind. Throughout this journey, I've also built an immense appreciation for my partner Ryan, my mother, and the support system of amazing women in my life.

AUTHOR'S NOTE

During my pregnancy journey, I loved learning about how my baby Harper was developing inside me and how my body was changing. There are so many books, blogs, podcasts, videos, and other resources for an expecting mom to learn about her baby's development, her body's changes during pregnancy, what to fill a nursery room with, and how to curate the perfect registry list. I felt very prepared with all the safety classes we took and the hours and hours of research I had done for everything we bought so that Harper would be comfortable when she entered our world. What I didn't know was what to expect after I was done "expecting" Harper—what to expect for when she was here in the world.

I had questions like:

- What will life be like with a newborn in the house?
- What is my body going to be like?
- What will our routine look like?
- What do I do with a baby?

I knew sleep was going to be hard to come by. A few close friends mentioned the "fourth trimester" and how it was a difficult time after your baby arrived. But what about it was hard? What were the details?

Why did I receive pink "mommy diapers" from a mom friend at my baby shower when they were not on my registry? Why didn't I know how badly I would need those diapers? More importantly, why didn't I know the reasons behind why I needed them?

I knew and had everything Harper needed, but why was I not as prepared for my own needs? I was lucky to have friends who subtly prepared me by providing some of these items so they were available when the time came, but not everyone is that lucky.

I now have pregnant friends who are building registries and asking me for "new mom" advice. It didn't take me long to realize why I had not heard more about my needs in the fourth trimester. Some of the topics are awkward for people to discuss. Society has generally made the topic of women's bodily functions, like periods, breastfeeding, and postpartum needs, something we do not openly discuss. After seeing how incredible a woman's body is by watching it create another being, I believe we should be able to have very open conversations about our bodies, what they are capable of, and what they go through.

While I am totally OK telling my friends things like:

- "Your boobs will hurt and get lumpy the longer you go without expressing your milk. Get a breast massager with a warming function to help alleviate clogged ducts and prevent mastitis. It was a lifesaver for me."

- "You will need 'mommy diapers' because you will be leaking and bleeding for weeks after delivering. Get the pink ones with little bows that make you feel like you're at least cute while it's happening to boost your confidence. There is truly nothing like a pink diaper dance around the house to make you and your partner laugh."

Only some people are open to talking like that.

But why is that? Our bodies are truly incredible; why should we not talk about them? We grow a human, push it out of a much-too-small hole, and then are expected to bounce back in no time. Our bodies are celebrated and "cute" while we are pregnant, but they are not treated the same during the hardest part for us while we are healing, on a hormonal roller coaster, and learning how to be a mom.

It is time to talk about it. So, let's do just that!

Throughout this book, there are also sections of information for your support system, if you have one. During my pregnancy, it was hard to find educational materials for my husband Ryan to prepare him for our future. There were two main types of books I encountered:

1. **Picture books with big cartoon illustrations, bright colors, and short, bold sentences.** The books looked like those I had in Harper's baby library. My husband is not a child and, after reading the more than 600 pages of *What to Expect When You're Expecting*, I felt almost a little insulted that this was the caliber of book available for the support partner. Don't get me wrong, some of the images and blurbs were funny, but these books did not share the complexities of having a newborn.

2. **Books that had a narrative of the more traditional, old school father roles which conflicted with the loving, emotionally supportive partnership style we wanted.** Empathy is a crucial factor in a new mom postpartum and books that have a more macho tone or that do not truly showcase the mom's journey are not helpful.

Even the books I found that were somewhat helpful did not always apply to our situation or my personal needs. I ended summarizing the main points of the baby books I read, connecting those points to our partnership and parenting ideologies, and then talking through the themes and concepts with Ryan after I finished each chapter.

Your support partner for the fourth trimester may be your spouse like mine, or they could be family, friends, siblings, neighbors, or your community. Regardless of who makes up your postpartum community, you will want to prepare them for postpartum. Just like how I summarized the information for Ryan, I have included sections in this book specifically for your support system so that you can share or have them read the details about how to support you best.

You may be having one, two, three, or more babies. You may be opting for a natural birth or a C-section. You may be planning to deliver at home, in the hospital, in a birthing center, or even a bathtub. You might be all for breastfeeding, undecided about it or going the formula route. You may have a significant other, or you may be on your own. No matter your circumstances, you are probably a soon-to-be parent, and we have the beautiful journey to motherhood in common.

Speaking of motherhood, while I may refer to the birthing parent as "mom" or use feminine pronouns such as "she" and "her" throughout the book, this book is intended for anyone who is becoming a parent and navigating the challenges and joys of the postpartum period, regardless of gender identity or expression.

Just like all the other parenting tips you are likely getting from people you know, or random strangers who see (and even want to touch) your pregnant belly, you may not need or relate to every section of this book. Not every piece of advice is going to suit your style and that is expected. The goal is for you to learn what may happen postpartum and what options you have, and then use that information to be the best momma you can be.

This book is full of my personal experience of becoming a mom and struggling, surviving, and thriving through the fourth trimester. While I am not a medical professional and my experiences may be different from yours, I hope my journey helps you learn and prepare for some of what you may go through on your path through motherhood.

I wouldn't be doing this right if I didn't bring you into my girlfriend circle. We are going to chat just like I do with my other gal pals. While I may not have a glass of wine in hand while doing so (and you probably don't either!), we are going to "spill the postpartum tea." We are going to get into the juicy, sometimes gross, sometimes shocking details, and have some laughs along the way. You are probably going to learn more about me than you ever wanted to know. Think of this as a candid tell-all from your best mom friend who has been there before and won't let you go through it alone.

You ready? Let's chat!

CONTENTS

CHAPTER ONE

Welcome to the World, Little One

A*m I peeing myself?*

I'm standing over the trash can in my kitchen, 39 weeks pregnant, and there is warm liquid running down my legs three days before my scheduled induction date. A little squeeze "down there" confirms it is not, in fact, pee. If it was, I would be able to control the flow.

"My water just broke!" I exclaim to my husband Ryan. He looks up from his seat at the kitchen counter and immediately starts consulting our "It's Happening!" checklist.

I quickly hobble, legs squished together, to the bathroom while giggling like a child. The glee of being in labor, combined with the ridiculousness of leaking everywhere, is too hilarious not to laugh at!

On the flip side, Ryan is full-blown panicked.

"The car is packed. Our families are notified. What else do we need? Are you ready to go to the hospital?" he asks.

We can't go yet, though; we have essential things to do first.

"I need to vacuum the nursery. Can you please blow out the leaves in the garage really quick before we go?" I respond. "We have some time. I haven't even felt a contraction yet!"

I mean, I can't have our little, precious baby Harper come home to a room with dog hair on the floor. Ryan's expression and guttural sigh says otherwise.

"I Googled how long to wait to go to the hospital after your water breaks,' so we should be fine. Plus, most of our friends had lengthy labors, and we don't want to get there too early!"

Ryan shakes his head and goes to the garage.

I quickly change into comfy, dry leggings and finagle a mega-pad in place. Thankfully, someone gifted me a pack of super pads at my baby shower even though I hadn't added them to my registry. The pad is just plain massive, which is good considering what it needs to do. I assume that this is what it feels like to wear a diaper. I even have the weird waddle-walk to go with my extra-padded bum.

Halfway through my vacuuming session, Ryan walks into Harper's room. He finished loading out go-bags into the car and even blew out the garage for me. I could tell I reached the limit for him letting me "do my thing."

"Can you take a picture? We need to document this!" I say with a goofy smile to cut his stress-induced tension. Ryan cracks a smile too as I pose with the vacuum up against my massive belly.

I quickly finish cleaning and can sense his relief as we walk closer to the back door, each step increasing our likelihood of leaving. I have one foot over the threshold to the garage.

"Hold on. I need to grab something quickly!" I shout as I step back into the kitchen, grab my leftover pineapple curry and rice from the night before, and pop it into the microwave for 60 seconds. The timer goes off, and I sprint out the door and jump into our getaway car.

"In my pregnancy research, I read that you must get a good meal before labor as you might not eat in the hospital. I couldn't imagine labor on an empty stomach! Plus, I don't want to waste this curry. It's too good," I justify my lunch to Ryan with a grin.

"It's a good thing you're cute," Ryan responds, grinning back as he chauffeurs our almost family of three to the hospital.

I don't feel quite as cute as usual considering that I am still leaky. And it wasn't just one gush; my waters kept breaking for what felt like two hours.

Filled with pure excitement to meet Harper and satisfaction from a yummy lunch, we casually walk into the hospital for check-in. The process is easy, especially since I alerted the hospital that we were on the way, and I had pre-registered a few days prior, so they had my details handy.

After checking in, we leisurely follow the nurse to our newly renovated delivery room, where I anticipate we will spend quite a few hours. I change into a hospital gown. The nurses set me up in a comfy bed and hook me up to various monitors to hear Harper's heartbeat and gauge my contractions, which I haven't felt yet.

Ryan heads back home to take care of a few errands. I am only slightly dilated and have not felt contractions, so we have tons of time, right?

While Ryan is gone, I get comfortable before I text and FaceTime my friends and family, find a movie to watch, use the bathroom, and have a snack. My phone starts to vibrate.

"How's it going, babe?" Ryan asks.

"No changes! But I think you should come back soon. I don't want you away for too long," I reply. While nothing has changed, I have this funny feeling that Ryan needs to come back now. Like right now. If there is one thing I've learned throughout my 32 years, it is always to follow my intuition. I don't want to make Ryan nervous, so I keep my tone casual while ensuring he heads back ASAP.

Within 20 minutes of Ryan's return to our room, one of the nurses comes in with a faster pace than before. She checks the monitors on the wall as Ryan and I obliviously chat with her.

"A few more nurses will be joining us soon," she says in an un-alarming manner.

She starts messing with the monitors that track Harper's heartbeat in my belly. Five to six more medical staff enter the room. Even with all those people, it is surprisingly quiet. I realize the missing sound is Harper's heartbeat on the monitor.

"Little Harper is just being dramatic. We are just going to repo-sition you," one of the nurses says as she flips me onto one side and moves the monitor around to try to hear Harper's heartbeat.

"She's just playing around," says another nurse as she pushes on my belly to reposition Harper for a better listen.

At this point, ten plus people are in the room, including one of the doctors in my OBGYN's practice. My actual OBGYN was not avail-able, and I had not met this new doctor.

"Hi. I am Doctor I-Can't-Remember-Her-Name. Harper is excit-ed to come out. I am going to try touching her head to get her moving. Are you okay with that?"

Am I okay with that? This stranger is telling me that she needs to put her hand right on up inside of me to tickle Harper's head without any form of anesthetic. All this is happening so fast, and I do not know what to feel. All the team has told me so far are platitudes to keep me calm instead of real information. I have full confidence in the medical team, and I don't want to get in their way with my questions, so I don't ask any. I let them do what they need to do to deliver Harper safely. I don't feel scared, just emotionally numb.

I nod, say "yes" to the doctor, and open my legs. Considering I am not dilated, it is very uncomfortable and painful. My focus quickly shifts to the signs of relief shown by the staff as the heartbeat monitor "beeps" into a consistent pattern.

"There she is!" says the doctor as she removes her glove. "We do not want Harper to give us a scare again. We recommend an emergency C-section right now."

Without a moment of hesitation, I say, "Let's go."

I look at Ryan, and he is in shock. Even though we are both wearing masks due to Covid protocol, I can see the fear in his eyes and try to relay strength over fear through mine.

The staff starts rolling my bed out of the room.

"Ryan, I love you!" I yell.

I am about to go through a major surgery, and I need him to hear it one more time. I have an underlying blood clotting disorder which makes any surgery risky. There is a small chance I may not come back. With that terrifying thought, I am compelled to remind Ryan, through all the chaos, that I love him.

On the way to the OR, we pass by a bunch of pizza boxes on a table for the hospital staff.

"Can I grab a to-go slice for Harper and me?" I ask and hear a few chuckles from my medical team as the OR doors burst open.

My confidence in the medical team continues to increase as they expertly talk me through everything they are doing.

"We have done this a million times before. We are just moving at light speed for you, just in case," they explain.

A male nurse sits me up on the bed, directs my legs over the edge, and prepares my back for the epidural as I shake uncontrollably. The adrenaline is pumping through me, and while I feel calm knowing I am in good hands, I hug the nurse in front of me for stabilization and general support. I start to hyperventilate and cry a little. I don't know why my body is reacting like that while my mind is numb. The nurse hugs me and tells me I am doing an excellent job.

I am surprised that the epidural doesn't hurt, but that could be because of all the adrenaline. I lay on my back, breathing deeply to stay calm while the team works. I use my voice to remind my team of the two medical conditions they need to be aware of for my surgery. They tell me they are prepared and that I am in good hands.

Before I realize it, Ryan is in the room. He is in blue scrubs to match his mask. He holds my hand. I feel so much better with him by my side.

The anesthesiologist lightly pushes on my lower stomach.

"Ouch! That hurt!" I exclaim as he pinches my arm, hard.

"I pinched your stomach twice as hard," he responds.

I am immediately relieved at how quickly and effectively the drugs kick in!

"We are beginning the incision."

The doctors open me up and talk us through what they are doing. I just make "mhmm" noises, squeeze Ryan's hand, and try to take deep breaths. I don't feel anything from my chest down.

"Get out your phone and start snapping!" the nurse behind me tells Ryan.

Ryan stands up and angles his phone over the blue separation sheet between my chest and the surgery area.

"Look!" I hear the doctor say.

I adjust my gaze in their direction, and there she is. My perfect, six-pound four-ounces, baby girl. The doctor raises her up, Simba over Pride Rock style, above the divider. She is an odd yellow color and covered in gook, but I don't care. She is alive, precious, and mine.

The nurses take Harper to the back to get cleaned up and usher Ryan over to join them. They wrap her up, put on a little white bow, and quickly bring her over to me. They place her in my arms, and I can't believe she is ours. I feel a rush of emotions, the main ones being relief, love, joy, and pride.

While I thought this was the finish line, after 39 weeks, three trimesters of pregnancy, I was wrong. This was the moment when the fourth trimester started.

CHAPTER TWO
You Did It! Now What?

Iremember the operating room. I somewhat remember being wheeled out to our birthing suite where Harper was supposed to come out "the natural way." I remember watching Ryan and the nurse across the room look at Harper on the medical table where they weighed her, counted her fingers and toes, took measurements, and confirmed she was "perfect." Ryan kept looking back at me with this "I am totally smitten" face every few minutes and yelling updates over his shoulder so I could hear from across the room.

I remember the elevator doors opening as our family of three was moved to our tiny little room that would be our home for the next few days. I remember being propped up on the hospital bed, with my massive, hospital-provided, bendy straw water cup in hand, being so tired but so happy we were safe.

I do not remember much of our first night in the hospital. The little details, the conversations, and how my body felt were all a blur. I only know what happened from Ryan's memory or the pictures he took as I was too exhausted to take in anymore.

No matter what kind of birth you had—in the hospital, at a birthing center, at home, or even in the back of a car—giving birth is a whirlwind experience. Once you have accomplished the incredible feat of bringing your baby into this world, have completed all the health checks, and are staring down lovingly at the babe nestled on your chest, what happens next?

Your most important responsibilities that trump all else as a new parent are threefold:

1.   Nurture your baby.
2.   Heal your body and mind.
3.   Learn as much as you can.

These same responsibilities hold true for your partner as well. To be as prepared as possible to do these three things, it is important to know what you are going through both physically and mentally. Let's dive right in!

Physical State

So, you just had a baby. Let's talk about your current physical state.

No matter where or how you gave birth, you are coming down from an insane amount of adrenaline from either all that intensive pushing or going through a C-section. Your labor might have been quick, or it may have lasted for days. The emotions of childbirth are plentiful. Excitement, nerves, confidence, insecurity, exasperation, fear, relief, love, joy; the birthing experience is a rollercoaster that your adrenaline will help you get through.

While I was giddy and joyful when my water broke, the emergency C-section, combined with a blood disorder that causes issues with clotting, made me pretty scared during the whole event. Relief was one of the most prominent emotions I felt coming out on the other side. There are so many emotions experienced during this time, so recognizing each one and acknowledging that any and all feelings are perfectly normal will help you along this path. Embrace your feelings, let your partner and care team know how you feel, and take some deep breaths to process everything you experienced.

Your babe may have arrived quickly, taken a few hours, or decided they wanted to stay put way longer than expected. Regardless, you will be exhausted.

You have at least one massive wound to heal. Women must deliver two things: the baby and the placenta. Another amazing fact about our bodies: women can grow a completely new organ through the pregnancy process—the placenta. The placenta attaches to the uterine wall and is where the umbilical cord stems from. It also provides the oxygen and nutrients the baby needs to grow and removes waste from the baby's blood (Mayo Clinic, Postpartum care, 2022). When you give birth to your child, your placenta detaches from the inner lining of your uterus. If you have a vaginal birth, you will continue to have contractions until the placenta is delivered, which can take around 20 minutes or so. If you have a C-section, the placenta is removed during the procedure.

Once the placenta detaches, you have an extensive wound inside your uterus that needs healing. While you had the luxury of evading your period for the past nine months, the wound and healing process produces a period-like blood, called lochia, that you will see over the next few weeks. Lochia mainly consists of blood, amniotic fluid, the tissue from your uterine lining, and cervical mucus. Sounds lovely, right? This is where those mega pads and adult diapers will come in handy.

If you had a natural birth, you might have a vaginal tear known as a perineal laceration (Mayo Clinic, Postpartum care, 2022). These tears occur when the baby's head is too large for the vagina to stretch around as it goes through the vaginal opening. The tears can be small or can go all the way from your vagina through to your anal sphincter and into the rectum. Your doctors will have remedied minor tearing with stitches after delivery. For major tears, a more intensive procedure may need to be done in the OR.

These stitches will need to heal over time, and there will be discomfort. Cold water and sitting on pillows may ease the recovery process. There are also ice pack pads that you can put in your underwear to help with swelling. They have a sticky side to help them stay in place, and once you pop the inner bag, the pad becomes nice and chilly. While I didn't need them for my lady bits, given I had a C-section, I did stick the sticky side to my sweatpants and use them on my healing incision. Either way, ice packs make you more comfortable. While items like ice pack pads may seem extravagant or excessive, after what you just went through, you should treat yourself as much as you want and make yourself as comfortable as possible.

If you had a C-section, you have a four- to six-inch-long incision across your lower belly that goes all the way through your abdomen and your uterus, through which your baby is delivered. This will likely make it challenging for you to move. You cannot engage your core muscles (abdomen) because they just underwent a major procedure. Any movement that causes abdominal muscle contraction is basically off-limits in the first few days. Walking around, standing, and even sitting up on your own will be an arduous task.

These limitations can be quite the conundrum. How are you supposed to take care of all the new mom responsibilities when you can't get up and down? My hospital bed was nice because it had a remote up/down function, so the bed would sit me up with limited use of my core. Fast-forward three days to my bed at home. Even though it was low to the ground, I couldn't just sit up and get up. I had to swing my leg, with quite a bit of force I might add, to roll myself over onto my belly, and crawl backwards off the bed to get out. Did it work? Yes. Was it sexy? Eh, with enough confidence, you can pull anything off, right?

Post-cesarean, you are also advised not to lift more than 10 pounds for four to eight weeks while you heal. While that weight limit may sound reasonable, it quickly becomes problematic. Your baby may weigh less than ten pounds, but when you add on the car seat and diaper bag, the weight quickly adds up. Make sure to have help, a stroller, and to prioritize what really needs to be in your diaper bag.

You may feel the lingering effects of medication from an epidural or spinal anesthetic, like nausea, fatigue, dizziness, and numbness or tingling in your extremities. Those feelings can be disorienting.

I couldn't feel my legs for what seemed like hours after the C-section. It could have been shorter than that, I do not really remember the timeline, but I do remember having this massive grin on my face once I could wiggle my toes again. From my hospital bed, I excitedly looked at my husband and exclaimed, "Look what I can do!" as my toes moved just a little bit as if that was just as impressive as having just birthed a baby! It's the little things that spark joy, right?

Your boobs might feel full, achy, and ready to start their careers as milk producers, even if you do not intend to breastfeed. You might even leak a little colostrum. Colostrum is the thick, very yellow milk that comes in first. It is jam-packed with nutrients for your baby and is much thicker than the milk that will come in over the following days.

Girlfriend, you just went through A LOT. Childbirth is not easy. Social media may make it seem like a breeze, but that is not 99% of the reality. Know that you are incredible and strong just for getting through this part. Your body is strong, too, and it knows how to heal you. You need to give it the time and rest to let it do its job (easier said than done, I know!).

Mental State

While your body has the task of healing, your mind has the task of assessing and working through your mental state.

Exhaustion and crashing hormones/adrenaline will have a major influence on your emotions. You may have feelings of joy and relief with bouts of happy, tired tears. You may be nervous or stressed about what to do next with your little bundle of joy who you are now responsible for throughout the rest of your life. You may be overwhelmed, depressed, or, in some cases, not feel bonded to the little one you just brought into this world. While movies, TV shows, and social media lead us to believe that we'll all bond with our babies immediately, the truth is for some, the bonding process takes time. If you do not feel bonded right away, you might feel like something is wrong with you but, spoiler alert: there's nothing wrong with you at all. All these emotions can happen for a short or long period of time and are all perfectly normal.

Read that again: **your emotions, whatever they are, are perfectly normal.**

After we were out of the OR and into the first room where they checked Harper over, I just remember feeling calm and completely in love. Harper was the perfect little mixture of Ryan and me. Even now, what I felt and still feel for her is hard to put into words. In addition to that, I fell more in love with Ryan. The way he was reacting to her, just completely in awe that we could make such a wonderful little thing, I knew he would be the best dad and partner throughout this journey.

On the other side of those feelings, though, I was filled with frustration since I couldn't sit up without pain or assistance due to my C-section. I was also totally and completely exhausted. I couldn't physically take care of myself. How would I take care of this little baby when I was such a mess?

I had the "Baby Blues" right after we got home from the hospital. I felt overwhelmed. While I knew I would establish a routine, eventually get more sleep, and heal, I questioned if I could ever put myself through this again. How do other women so happily pump out multiple babies when this was the experience afterwards? I wanted my "village" around me, but I felt so much pressure just trying to communicate my needs. While I tried to stay positive, I was not my usual upbeat, "I can do it" self. I cried, a lot.

The Baby Blues are feelings of sadness, anxiety, and mood changes in the few days after having a baby. Around 70-80% of new moms experience the Baby Blues (American Pregnancy Association). They start during the first few days postpartum and can last up to two weeks.

You may think you are going crazy, that you can't do it, that it is overwhelming. Billions of moms have had those same thoughts before you, and they, like you, were strong enough to overcome, heal, and love their little ones. So much so that many of those women had another baby after their first, and some have had three, four, five, six, and even seven+ babies. The emotions you feel are all part of it; they will improve, and you will survive.

If you experience a downturn in your emotional state postpartum, there are a few tricks to help you turn your spirits around:

- **Communicate how you are feeling with those around you.** They will help you more than you know. All you need to do is ask for help.

- **Get some fresh air.** Research shows that being outside and seeing greenery or water can improve your mood and energy levels. I took Harper outside to feed on our patio often and, once I was able, took her for walks around the neighborhood. Those moments of sunshine and fresh air helped tremendously.

- **Set small goals for what you want to accomplish each day.** It may seem like the tasks are never-ending. Prioritize the most essential and let the little things go.

- **Take time for self-care.** Even if that time is just five minutes for a shower, doing your make-up, or putting on "real" clothes for the day, do it. Trust me, you need it more than you know.

- **Make sure you are eating and drinking enough.** You aren't yourself when you're hungry, especially with all the extra calories and water you need.

- **Take a break from social media.** Social media comparison can easily lead to feelings of inadequacy. Remember, Instagram is not reality! Each mom's journey is different so don't compare yourself to others.

It is also important to recognize the difference between Baby Blues and Postpartum Depression—a more serious condition where seeking the support of your family and medical assistance is important.

If you have Baby Blues that last longer than two weeks and you still don't feel like yourself, you may have Postpartum Depression (PPD). Centers for Disease Control and Prevention (CDC) research indicates that one in eight women experience postpartum depression symptoms after pregnancy, and those are just from cases reported (Depression Among Women, 2023).

PPD can be detrimental to both mom and baby, and the symptoms do not always go away without help. Symptoms include (CDC, Depression Among Women, 2023):

- Crying more often than usual
- Withdrawal from those around you
- Not feeling connected to your baby
- Feelings of anxiety and stress, both physically and emotionally
- Not feeling like you are a good mom or able to care for your baby
- Not eating or sleeping
- Having thoughts of hurting yourself or the baby

PPD can last anywhere from a few days to several months. Treatment for PPD can often include psychotherapy, mental health counseling, anti-anxiety medication, and anti-depressant medication (Mayo Clinic, Postpartum Depression, 2023).

The CDC also reports that new parent partners can experience depression after their baby has arrived (Depression Among Women, 2023). Check in with your partner frequently not only about how you are feeling, but also about how they are feeling.

If you feel that your symptoms are similar to those above or that your mental state is deteriorating, be vocal about it. All your emotions are normal and seeking help to work through your emotions is normal as well. Asking for help is vital to ensure you are supported through this major physical and emotional transition.

Be open and honest about your mental and emotional state with your support system. Whether that system includes your medical team, friends, family, community groups, or therapist, they are there to help. While your medical team knows your physical needs, they will only know your mental state if you tell them. If you ask for help, your team will equip you with the tools you need to be the best mom you can be. Remember, there is absolutely no shame in the emotions you feel. You are not alone in this, as so many women before you have had the same thing.

The most significant takeaway for the days, weeks, and months after you give birth is to be open with others and ask your support system for help with anything and everything you need. There is nothing you can ask, say, or do that your nurses, doctors, Doulas, therapist, or birthing team have not heard or seen before. Make sure you tap into all they have to teach you so you can learn to be the best mom you can be.

The Milk Factory

Breastfeeding does not come as naturally to most women as you might think. There are different angles and positions to consider, the baby may have a tongue or lip tie, which can make it difficult for them to latch, or your nipples might be bigger or smaller than the baby can use at the moment. Breastfeeding can be a lot of trial and error and just be, well, complicated.

On day one, I thought Harper was latching, and we were successfully breastfeeding. On day two, we discovered Harper was not, in fact, latching and, therefore, not feeding. I used the hospital pumps to get colostrum out and fed it to Harper through a tiny syringe when she needed to eat. I tried many different positions but was not having luck latching Harper to my breast. Both Harper and I were getting frustrated.

A friend had told me to use the lactation consultants as much as possible, and we had already seen two consultants within the first 24 hours. At 3 AM on night two, I knew we needed to get this right. Even though we were exhausted, I requested another consult to try other strategies.

The lactation consultant arrived around 3:20 AM and walked me through various positions. She then suggested a nipple shield—a wide-brimmed hat-looking plastic piece that goes over your nipple and areola. The nipple shield suctions onto the nipple, making it easier for the baby to latch. It worked within two attempts, and Harper was chowing down!

I saw the milk filling the nipple shield and Harper sucking it out. I was so tired but thrilled and relieved we could make it work! Ryan was cheering us on at my bedside. I don't know when we would have figured out breastfeeding on our own had I not been so adamant about getting help and asking as many people as possible. Three AM on night two did the trick, and I am so glad that worked. The squeaky wheel gets oiled, or in this case, the squeaky mom gets milked!

There are many emotions tied to breastfeeding and the ability or inability to do it successfully. The world puts so much pressure on moms to be perfect and suggests that everything should work effortlessly. The assumption is that babies just latch on without issue and that the milk is just there, available, and ready to go, but that is not reality. Over 70% of mothers experience breastfeeding difficulties (Gianni, M. L., et al, 2019). Sometimes, like in my case, the baby has trouble latching. Sometimes, your body can have difficulty producing milk or you experience pain. All that can cause stress, pressure, and feelings of failure.

If you opt to breastfeed and it does not start out easily, know that you will figure it out, and you are certainly NOT a failure. The most important thing is that your baby is fed and loved. You will try your best to give them the nourishment they need, and if you must go with formula or with pumping to start, that is okay.

Every mom's journey is different, and your baby will love you no matter what or how many variations of feeding you use. You may feel guilty about an inability to latch, produce, or know what to do, but it is not something to feel guilty about. You cannot control those things, and they are not your fault. What you can control is how you reach out to that support system to help you get your little one fed.

What is Sleep?

Sleep will be hard to come by in the few days after giving birth. You will have a schedule of things that rotate every two and a half to three hours for the entire 24 hours of your day between the baby's naps, diaper changes, feeds, awake times, and more naps. In those moments when you are not working through that routine or loving on your babe, you may also be pumping, getting a visit from a nurse or doctor, trying to eat your own food, talking to loved ones, or taking a trip to the restroom that rivals the amount of time my husband usually takes.

You may be surprised to learn that babies are very loud sleepers! Harper made so many funny noises throughout the night. As a new mom, I was on high alert for any little sound, so having Harper sleep in our room meant I could not fall into a deep sleep. With every noise, I woke up, looked at her, and made sure she was still my perfect, tiny tater tot. I just didn't know tater tots could grunt like that!

If you are in the hospital, know that those nurse and doctor visits are also not coordinated. They may come in groups, back-to-back, or randomly throughout the day. Their visits will make sleep difficult, so you can ask them to try and consolidate visits if possible. You will not have all the hospital staff's help at home. Use them to help you find time to recover.

You should also check your hospital's sleep arrangement offerings. We were fortunate that our hospital offered both in-room and nursery options for Harper's care. While separating from our child within the first 72 hours of her life outside the womb was emotionally challenging and guilt-inducing, we used the hospital's baby room the first two nights in the hospital. We were able to get two to three much-needed hours of interruptions-free, deeper sleep. The nurses took Harper down to their observation room around 9 PM and came back every two and a half to three hours for feeding. Once she came for her 7 AM feed, she stayed for the rest of the day.

I am a big sleeper and usually get eight to nine hours a night. I know that without sleep, I am not my best self nor the best mom I can be. Getting a few hours to recuperate was crucial to my mental and physical healing. The importance and repercussions of good sleep made using the hospital resources a much easier decision. Even though it was only for a few hours at a time, the rest we got was so helpful in the recovery process! While not every hospital or birthing center has options for sleeping arrangements, it is worth looking into all your birthing locations' offerings and policies so you can use them accordingly.

Your body is going through a momentous change and healing process, so rest is critical at this stage. Your phone and social media will be there when you wake up or go home. Try to sleep during any time you have for yourself in those early days and know that this stage is temporary. You will get more sleep eventually.

Potty Training, for You!

Between day two and day three, you will be asked to start using the restroom and may potentially have your first bowel movement. The first "number two" can come within 24 hours to five days of having your baby (Mayo Clinic, Postpartum care, 2022). Drinking plenty of water will help prevent constipation from dehydration. Also, if you have not heard the advice to start taking laxatives a few days before your due date, listen to it now. The first poop can be scary!

You just had significant changes "down there," and all your intestines are moving back into place after being cramped for months. You may also have hemorrhoids after birth. Hemorrhoids are swollen veins within the anus, caused by increased pressure, and they can cause swelling, bleeding, and itching in your bottom. Women who give birth naturally frequently get hemorrhoids given all the pressure from pushing and the baby. In time, they will go away on their own, but staying hydrated, using stool softeners, eating a high-fiber diet, ice packs or cold water, and resting will help to speed up the process (Osborn, 2018).

On the bright side, you get to wear some *super sexy* new garments for the next few weeks: adult diapers, mega pads, and full-coverage, high-rise panties. A Peri bottle, also known as a portable bidet, will also be your new best friend. Peri bottles are squirt bottles with an angled sprayer to soothe and clean your healing wounds. There is nothing like the sweet relief of cold water on your nether bits when you are stiff and swollen, and it is hard to do anything down there.

When the time comes, it will be hard to make your way to the bathroom, sit down on your porcelain throne, and do your thing. Just take your time, and don't push too hard.

Hospital Hacks

Outside of the first loo adventure and loving on your baby, quite a few other things are happening during your stay. You may have seen online parody videos of all the attendants checking in on you every few hours. Some come all at once or in stages, but you will have lots of visitors. They also come when you try to nap or sleep, even if someone just left.

Although they may be annoying at points, the staff are excellent resources. They taught Ryan how to change Harper's first diaper. They taught us how to swaddle her, how to use the breast pump, how to feed, Harper's signs of hunger or sleepiness, how often to get up, and how to take care of myself. They took Harper's vitals, gave her the first vaccines, and helped us sign up for a Social Security number and a Birth Certificate. We relied on them and asked so many questions. I encourage you to do the same and write as much down as possible.

If the staff is comfortable with it, you can even take "how-to" videos for an easy reference once you are home. Swaddling, for example, is an art form, and your postpartum brain will not help you remember all the details of how to do it. Most of it will be a blur!

Ryan vividly remembers the lactation consultant teaching us how to use a manual breast pump. I found the pump four months later in our kitchen and asked Ryan what it was. I was surprised he knew all about it and how to use it. I was physically present and awake the entire time the nurse showed both of us in the hospital room but have zero memory of that!

With that said, try to document everything. Yes, you need to note the important details the doctors tell you, but outside of that, take photos and videos of all the big and small moments of you and your new little one. They grow so fast, and you will likely rewatch and look at those moments hundreds of times over the first few months of their life. I wish we had taken more, especially videos, as they were so precious, and she was so tiny.

If you have a loved one staying with you during your stay, the living conditions may be uncomfortable. Unless you splurge for a room upgrade, get ready for an awkward sleeping situation on a small couch or bed. Ryan was on a small, hard couch. His six-foot-two-inch body did not fit right on that five-and-a-half-foot-long couch. Make the best of the situation by bringing your pillow, comfortable clothes, and slippers.

After just a few short days of becoming a parent, you will eventually have to leave your cocoon and safely net of the hospital. On the way out, take everything with you. Pack your goodie bag with all the pads, diapers, bottles (Peri and water), nipple creams, nipple shields, baby onesies, massive water cup, swaddles, and any other goodies that the hospital gave you for your little one. If you or your insurance paid for it, take it!

Make sure you know how to put your baby in the car seat. Ryan and I had yet to test that out, and with new-mom-fog-brain and his lack of sleep, we tried to put the straps on in the weirdest, most incorrect way possible. Thankfully, a nurse showed us how to strap in our bundle of joy correctly! With that delay, packing up, the last few doctor checkups, and soaking in the last few moments of supported parenting before we were out on our own, we were rolled out in a wheelchair to our car about three hours later than we had planned.

Once the car seat was in place securely and our seat belts were clicked in, both Ryan and I let out big sighs. We made it through the first three days of parenthood with the security blanket of the hospital staff covering us. Leaving the parking garage meant we were on our own. We looked at each other with a mix of relief, excitement, exhaustion, and confidence that we could do this. Ryan put the car in reverse, and we were off!

For Your Partner

From Ryan's perspective, once my water broke, he had to balance his pregnant wife deciding to vacuum when we should have been going to the hospital, getting our go-bags into the car, and knowing when to say, "That's enough, we've got to go!" At home and during the drive to the hospital, he came off to me as calm and collected, but in his head, he was yelling at his crazy wife that blowing out leaves in the garage was not, in fact, our priority. Those things were insignificant to his goals of getting us safely into the hands of our qualified care before any problems arose. Thankfully, we had done a practice run to the hospital prior to the big day, so Ryan knew exactly where the parking garage was for expecting parents.

Once we were all set up in the hospital room for delivery, Ryan left the hospital to pick my car up from the car wash. I had just come home from dropping my car off before my water broke, and we couldn't leave the car at the wash for three days. Ryan got my car, tended to the dogs before my sister arrived to watch them, and picked up a few more items we needed.

Ryan was trying to be quick. Picking up my car was not worth missing the birth of our child. When I told him to hurry back, he was excited. While he was nervous about becoming a dad, he was also "super pumped." Not only that, but our room had a massive, brand new reclining chair right in front of a big screen TV where he planned to watch basketball in the hours of waiting ahead of us. The baby and basketball combo were a win-win in his book.

Once all the chaos started, Ryan watched, not knowing how to help, as the doctors did their thing. He watched my eyes and knew my expression under my Covid-protocol mask was one of concern and fear. He was so used to my usual "it's going to be fine" attitude that seeing me scared sent him into a panic.

Ryan didn't want to get in the way either and didn't know how to help or what to do. When the doctors announced that it was time for an emergency C-section, one of the nurses threw scrubs in his direction and told him to get dressed for when they would come and grab him to go to the operating room in five minutes or so.

Ryan had never been as scared in his entire life. He was all alone in a silent room after ten minutes of chaos. He called his parents and then FaceTimed mine, who reached out to my Auntie Jenny, a NICU nurse , in Australia. My parents put the phones up to one another, and

Jenny walked Ryan through what was happening and what to do since all ten people who were in the room had left with me to the OR.

Once he was brought to the OR, Ryan was relieved to see me and hold my hand. While he didn't want to watch the surgery, given how gory it is, he tried to give me updates on what was happening. Ryan was amazed at how well and how quickly my medical team worked together.

Upon instruction from the nurse, Ryan held the camera up over the surgical drape and took pictures of Harper as she was brought into this world. While Ryan is not the photographer in our relationship, those were the best photos we could have asked for. He even took a picture of the clock at the time she was born, 3:03 PM. The video of our swaddled Harper being placed in my arms for the first time as I said "hello" still pulls at my heartstrings, no matter how many times I watch it.

When they placed Harper in Ryan's arms, he was flooded with emotions. At first, he was overwhelmed, and the weight of our new life hit him.

"We now have a child. She is our responsibility for the rest of our lives," he thought.

He was also in shock and a bit traumatized by everything that had happened over the last hour. We went from zero contractions to a medical scare to a full-on baby arrival in an hour, and there was no time to think or process during any of it.

Once Ryan held Harper, he broke down. He thought, "Wife is okay. Baby is okay. Now, I can breathe."

Holding her for the first time. Looking down at her perfect little face, made even cuter by a tiny gauze bow the nurse had made for her.

Seeing her take her first breaths. Ryan realized that "Harper was me and my wife. The best parts of us together." He was totally in love.

We were eventually moved to our tiny hospital room where we would spend the next three days. Ryan was too scared to go to sleep when Harper went to bed for the first time. He was terrified of Harper not eating enough. She was so tiny, and he was so big. He didn't want to hurt her. Overall, Ryan never had a baby before and hadn't been around kids often, so he didn't know what to expect and was not confident as a new parent.

The days went by very fast. Ryan did get some relief as he left the hospital to get food occasionally or go home to make sure the dogs were okay. He felt that it was a guilty pleasure to get out and get fresh air and not to be stuck in the room for three days. It was also stressful though as we had Harper during the Covid crisis. There were so many checkpoints to get in and out of the hospital. Walking down the halls, Ryan passed so many rooms with red paper all over the door, indicating that the patients in that room had Covid. We had to wear masks when any doctors or nurses entered the room and were worried that we or Harper may contract Covid from those nearby.

Ryan also felt empathy for me. I couldn't move, use the restroom, or do anything. I am such a strong person and seeing me at my weakest was hard. It broke his heart that Harper struggled to latch and the repercussions that had on my confidence as a mom. He thought I was doing an amazing job but knew I was not being as successful as I wanted to be.

Overall, Ryan's experience of becoming a new father was filled with panic, shock, fear, and relief, but it ended in unconditional love and pure joy.

Once Harper was in the world, Ryan had to figure out how to be a father and step up as a partner. I was focused on feeding and recovering with limited mobility. I needed Ryan to focus on everything else.

Your Mental State

Congratulations! You have also just become a parent. While you may not have been the one to grow and birth your child, you have done the job of being the supportive partner. Upon arrival, you may be feeling the following:

- Total joy and excitement
- Relief that your partner and child are alright
- A final realization that you are now becoming a parent
- Total and unconditional love for your new little one and your partner
- Fear or worry that you do not know what to do next or how to support your partner
- Uncomfortable with your little baby and a sense of unease about what to do next
- Fear of holding this tiny, fragile little baby as they need so much support

Just like your partner, all your feelings and emotions are valid. The good thing is that the birthing center, Doula, or hospital staff can and will support you too, with their wealth of information. Don't be afraid to ask, ask a second time, confirm a third, and maybe get shown again for a fourth time. You will be sleep deprived and tired, and now is the time to lean on those around you to learn and grow your confidence.

On top of learning everything you can, your two main priorities are:

1. Supporting your partner as they recover and learn to be a parent. Showing up for your partner by demonstrating your want to co-parent and support in these first few days will strengthen your relationship and build trust throughout your parenting journey together.

2. Developing your bond with your baby.

Supporting Momma

You and the mom-to-be may have a solid and comfortable routine for communication, how you show up for one another emotionally, and how you split chores and tasks. Having that foundation built is a great start to preparing how your relationship and roles will evolve with a baby. The baby and all their needs will add new emotional, physical, time, and task pressures for both of you.

Strategies that worked pre-baby may not work post-baby. If you and your partner have a system that relies on one of you asking the other to do something when it needs to be done, it's best not to assume that will be the case now. Let go of household expectations you had pre-baby and embrace a more relaxed state of things, at least for now. Do what absolutely needs doing but be content with some tasks not getting done. Start having conversations now about responsibilities and how you both will tackle situations together so that you both are prepared for when the baby comes.

Since you both will be sleep deprived and likely to forget items, perhaps now is the time to map out a task chart—even if you've never used one before! This ensures that what needs to get done does and that there are no communication misunderstandings.

Once the baby is here, it is time to put those conversations and task charts into practice. You will also likely be brain-dead tired and you may not know where to start. If that is the case, when in doubt, just DO.

After having a baby, the mental load of managing all that needs to be done and making decisions can be stressful and exhausting for the new mom. In addition to that, they may experience the Baby Blues or Postpartum Depression. Having a supportive partner who takes on the mental tasks of deciding what needs to be done and doing those things is an incredible relief. Try to anticipate your partner and baby's needs and do as much as possible to fulfill them.

You may already play this role in your relationship now and plan to do this when the baby is here. Since your life will look a little different when baby arrives, here are some hands-on ideas of what task help can look like once baby is here:

- Clean and fill up mom's water bottle when it is empty. She is going to be very, very thirsty and needs to stay hydrated.
- Take charge of bottle, pump part, and binky cleaning duties.
- Change the baby's diaper (especially when mom is sleeping).
- Learn how to swaddle your munchkin and help put them to bed.
- Change the baby's clothes after a spit-up session. Don't worry if the outfit you pick doesn't match. It's the thought that counts!
- Make sure diapers and wipes are always in stock and order more when they are out.
- Clean up the trash or toys around the room.

- Manage where all the paperwork is stored.
- Learn how all their clothes are organized so you can help with laundry and putting that laundry away.
- Make sure any pets are cared for.
- Cook meals (or order / pick them up).
- Make sure mom has eaten. She is going to need snacks. Lots and lots of snacks.

You may be unsure how to do some of your new responsibilities sometimes or feel uncomfortable doing them. Those feelings of unease are perfectly normal. When in doubt, communication is key. All you need to do is ask for your partner's opinion or guidance.

That communication comes in handy when making big decisions—like what to eat for dinner. That question popped up for us every night, around 4:30 or 5:30 PM. Our stomachs would start to rumble, and since we were off our normal routine, we usually didn't have dinner planned out.

Do we cook something? What do we have? Do we need to run to the store? Do we eat out? Does that mean takeout or a sit-down restaurant? What type of food do we want?

These all seem like relatively easy questions, but they frequently caused me to panic.

When do I need to pump next? Can I pump while cooking? When does Harper need to go down for bed or feed next? What would I dress her in, or myself, if we went out into the world? Gosh, does that mean I need to do my hair and put on makeup? Do I have time to do that? If we go sit in a restaurant, that also means I need to pack the diaper bag and prep a bottle. Does the diaper bag have diapers and a change of clothes?

The questions kept coming, and I got overwhelmed. Why? Because it was one more thing I had to decide with too many options that came with many other questions. We both needed to eat, and I just wanted (and needed) Ryan to make the overall decision (like "we are going out for dinner") and maybe ask for advice or my opinion on a smaller piece ("Thai or pizza?"). That way, I only had to plan for one scenario and could more easily move forward.

But I hadn't communicated that to Ryan prior to Harper's arrival, so we were using our pre-baby communication strategies. Trying to explain to him the question spiral in my head was very difficult.

Being in the midst of sleep deprivation and baby spit-up is not the time to have a "Let's talk about our communication style" with your partner. Take my advice: sort that stuff out before baby comes and come up with guidelines. Those guidelines will relieve some of the mental burden for both of you and will help you develop an even closer relationship as a team in this phase of your newborn's life.

In addition to the physical task help, your partner will also need emotional support.

Be kind to the new momma. They are likely very vulnerable right now about their body, how it looks, and the fact that strangers are seeing and poking all parts of it. They may be sensitive to others, including you, seeing them in their changing body as well. Tell them your genuine feelings about how beautiful their body is, how strong it is, and how you will support them as they recover. Be appreciative of how much of their body and mind they have sacrificed and will still sacrifice for your new bundle of joy. While it may have taken two to make the baby initially, the burden of growing your baby and, if they are breastfeeding, now feeding your baby is theirs to bear.

Your partner's hormones are also all over the place, so they may be very emotional. Be aware of those emotions, don't take things personally, be patient with them, and love / support them. Listen to their needs and do as much as possible to alleviate some of that stress. Be the shoulder they need when they cry, as they will likely cry often. In time, their hormones will level out, but they will still need you to be strong and consistent all the way through that process and afterward.

The first few months with a newborn are unlike any time period you will ever go through together again. It is a time to test your partnership and show your support for one another. Being present and supportive during this crucial time will make your bond even stronger, build respect for one another as you've never had before, and give you the confidence that, together, you can get through anything.

Baby Bonding

While your partner has been feeling your baby grow inside of them for months, you have probably only experienced some kicks, a hiccup here and there, and seen the growth of your partner's belly. Up until this point, it may be harder for your impending parenthood to feel real or for you to feel as excited as they are. Once the baby is here, it is a whole different ball game! You can now hold, see, and love on your little nugget of joy.

A very important part of the bonding process is skin-to-skin contact (also known as cuddling). Skin-to-skin holding is when the baby is lightly clothed, in basically just their diaper, and lays on you or your partner's bare chest with a blanket covering both of you. According to Stanford Health, this type of cuddling with your newborn has multiple benefits (2023):

- **Promotes Bonding:** It has been shown that, during skin-to-skin contact, both men and women release hormones and endorphins that promote feelings of love, closeness, and relaxation. These feelings are tied to your baby, which helps you develop love. Your baby will feel more relaxed and safer as they get to know you and your scent. It can also help you and your partner destress by reducing cortisol levels. Furthermore, skin-to-skin is shown to help reduce postpartum depression in women.

- **Body Temperature:** Babies have trouble self-regulating their body's temperature since they cannot shiver or add and subtract clothing as needed. During skin-to-skin contact, both the mom's and dad's bodies can adjust their body's temperature to the baby's to help your baby keep the correct temperature. Because the baby does not have to use as much energy to maintain their body temperature, it has a better chance of gaining weight and growing faster.

- **Developmental Benefits:** Skin-to-skin time has been shown to help the baby self-regulate their heartbeat and breathing patterns and can even help their digestion. Studies indicate that babies who receive skin-to-skin care have less pain and discomfort, so they tend to cry less often and fall into a deeper sleep. All these benefits also lead to improved brain development.

To make skin-to-skin time more accessible for Ryan, I bought him a super soft, warm robe. He would wear it around the house without a shirt underneath, and anytime he wanted to cuddle Harper, it was easy for him to put her on his chest under the warm robe. To this day, he still says it was the best gift he has ever gotten.

Bonding can take some time, and it is not always immediate. It can get frustrating. The easy way out is to do other things and go other places, but you would miss so much in your baby's life by doing that. Your baby needs you and your bond. Be intentional about your time with your baby and ensure quality time. Notate all the things they start to react to and look up their development stages so you can work on their growth. It is incredible to see them progress, even if it is just one small milestone at a time. While it may be slow, that bonding time is so essential for both of you, so don't give up!

Also, your baby may cry when they are handed to you, or they may reach for mom. That behavior does not mean that they do not love you or want to be with you. They are used to your partner's smell, warmth, and lack of facial and chest scruff. Their mom likely provides their food. Your baby's natural instinct is to be with their mother to survive.

Do not take their want to be with mom as a lack of love for you or that you are doing something wrong. That is not the case. It may take time, but as you build your bond together, your baby will reach for you, use you for warmth, take in your scent, and giggle at your funny faces. Know your bond will come with time, so don't take their natural instincts personally.

CHAPTER THREE

Home Sweet Home

Ryan's knuckles were white from squeezing the steering wheel so tightly on the drive home from the hospital. With such precious cargo in the car, it was the scariest drive of his life!

Bringing Harper home for the first time was a major milestone in our first week together. We were finally able to bond without the nurses and doctors interrupting. We introduced Harper to our dogs and to my sister, who had been dog sitting while we were in the hospital. After my sister left, we were able to get comfortable in our own space and finally experience our new family unit in our home, together. That first night felt like we took the hospital training wheels off and were finally on our own.

Whether you just brought your new baby home for the first time from your birthing center or you are through the first three days at home, you are going through a lot of changes. The good news is that you can do it. You have likely been preparing for months, nesting in the nursery, getting "all of the things" from your registry, and learning a lot.

Once you are home, it may feel like everything you learned has flown out of your brain. But guess what? You are surrounded by easy access to support. You have easy access to search the wealth of online resources on your phone or computer. You may have access to doctors via Teladoc or your appointments every few weeks after birth. You can call lactation specialists through your medical provider or free support services or hotlines. You can get almost anything and everything you need delivered right to your door, available for pick-up, lent from a friend, or found on a marketplace. Your friends and family around you will ask how they can help or are waiting to be told how they can support you.

While it might be hard to ask for help (it is a challenge for me), now is the time to lean on your community and support system. You will quickly learn who is there for you in rough times. You will learn that your friends, family, and community have gone through this before, and they are full of valuable tips and tricks. Don't be afraid to ask them for what you need!

Making Time for You

You will discover very quickly that your life now is on a timer. Your baby needs to wake up, have a diaper change, eat, stay awake for 30 to 45 minutes, and then sleep again within a two-and-a-half to three-hour rotation. You will also need to find time to eat, use the bathroom, shower, pump/breastfeed/give baby a bottle, and catch some sleep if you are lucky. The days go by quickly with this routine, and it can feel a little like Groundhog Day. Other chores need to be done, too, like maintaining your household, attending doctor appointments, and taking care of other kids or fur babies if you have those. The list piles up.

I have always been a doer with a go-go-go personality. I get things done. When I got home, I felt pressure to maintain the house and keep everything moving with Harper and me, even though I was still healing from my C-section. I had a ton of support from Ryan. He washed and sanitized bottles and all their parts, cleaned pump parts, took care of our dogs, and took care of me. I felt like I was not holding up my end of the work at some points, which was unequivocally false.

I was pumping and breastfeeding for Harper throughout the night and day while managing the "what", "how", and "when" of all the things that needed to get done on our list while battling three rounds of mastitis and trying to heal my incision. That was a lot. I learned that I needed to give myself grace. I was way too hard on myself with completely unrealistic pressure.

It was okay if the dishes stayed in the sink overnight or if the clothes were in a pile on the bed for a while. It was okay if I didn't shower for an extra day (or two) and wore sweatpants and comfy clothes for days on end. Who really cared if my neighbors saw me without makeup in mounds of comfy, mismatched clothes while walking our dog? All I was feeling was internal pressure for things that, at the end of the day, didn't matter.

After realizing my unwarranted guilt was causing me added stress, I knew I needed to change my mindset. I decided to do at least one "thing for me" every day. If that meant that one of my non-essential tasks dropped off, that would be okay with me. If Harper was fed, changed, and happy, I could also make myself happy.

Some days that looked like a long stroller walk outside or sitting on the patio reading while Harper napped. Some days that was a trip to Target without a list, just to shop (a dangerous game, I know). Some days it was getting five straight hours on the couch with Harper sleeping on my chest and watching Netflix because she was growing so fast, and soon, I wouldn't be able to do that anymore. Let me tell you, my "things for me" became some of the best memories I had with Harper and significantly helped my mental load. What I don't remember are the dishes left in the sink, the laundry I didn't put away, or any neighbors caring about my no-makeup face or mismatched outfits.

Give yourself grace during your time at home, and make sure to take time for yourself. Tasks will always be there, but the little moments that you can so easily take for granted won't.

Post-Baby Body

You may have been excited to "get your body back" once the baby emerged, but I regret to tell you that your body is not yet yours. Not for a long time. However, that is not a bad thing.

Let's set this up for the most exciting part—the cuddles. Baby snuggles are the best. Babies are like weighted blankets but 100% better. Just envision this warm, snuggly tater-tot curled up and asleep on your chest. They smell good, their hair tickles your chin, and they need you. They need you like no one has ever needed you in your whole life, and you are their whole world.

Those cuddles and that love will get you through the sleepless nights, the crying, the "hold-your-nose" level poopy diapers, and all the fluids that get thrown up on you. That love just becomes even more fun as they get older and develop a smile, laughter, and eventually say "Mama" for the first time.

Your body is there to sleep on, for comfort, for holding, for dancing, for hugs and squishes, climbing, and for a while if you decide, for nourishment. While your baby is no longer in your belly, they are still a part of you. Sometimes you will feel like you need space and time, and that is totally okay. Being needed that much can be a lot. You will likely be sharing your body with your babe longer than just the months of pregnancy. That's why it's crucial to find ways to make the demand for your body sustainable for your body and mind.

Outside of your little nugget clinging to your body, your body is going through some serious changes. Remember, you are still going to be healing for weeks "down there." That comes with a lot of leakages. You will likely be bleeding and expelling fluids for six to eight weeks (Cleveland Clinic, 2022).

I remember getting two packs of pink women's diapers with little black bows printed on them for my baby shower. I didn't register for those, and I didn't know how much I would need them until I got home. They were a life (and underwear) saver. Make sure you have a few packs of those and some mega pads ready for when you get home. You just went through a major bodily change and don't want to have to think about running to the store when you're just trying to get your new schedule down pat.

If you have a C-section, you will likely get your first good look at your wound a few days postpartum. For me, it was on day four after I had my first real shower at home. The doctors will bandage you up and provide wound care instructions, which will make you feel confident, but seeing that incision for the first time on your body is jarring. It will be angry red, potentially puffy, with a gnarly looking bruise. Remind yourself that it will heal and look better with time. My incision became infected, and I called my doctor right away to ensure it would still heal correctly with minimal scarring. Make sure to monitor your incision, don't push yourself, and keep your doctor up to date about any changes you notice in your healing process.

Eventually, the swelling and bruising will disappear, but you will always have a scar. Instead of making your scar a negative, try to change your mindset. I know that it is easier said than done. Seeing such a large scar can evoke many different emotions.

My scars are keloid. They are thick, raised off the skin, bumpy, and red. My incision scar stands out, and when I see it, I notice that I naturally frown. But then I think about what that scar means. That scar is where my baby came into this world. That mark on my body will forever show my sacrifice, hard work, commitment, and love for my child. I am proud of that scar. I earned every bit of what it stands for, and so did you.

With either a C-section or natural birth, a belly band or wrap can be quite helpful for extra support. Women have been wrapping their bellies for centuries after giving birth. Belly bands wrap tightly around your midsection to give your abdomen and back extra stability. Studies show that belly bands and wraps can help with pain, help your uterus shrink, help with Diastasis Recti by supporting your abdomen muscles, and support your pelvic floor muscles and your organs as they return to their pre-baby place (WebMd, 2023). Be sure to get the right size, especially with a C-section. If not, it could put pressure on your wound and cause issues with healing.

The sizing issue happened to me. I bought a belly band slightly larger than I would have used pre-baby. I didn't realize how big I would still be once Harper emerged. The band was tight, and when I wrapped it around me, it barely fit and was squeezing too much. Once I found the right size, about two sizes bigger than I initially bought, I used the belly band frequently for stabilization. It was very helpful in ensuring I did not engage my core too much when getting up and down off the couch or in and out of bed.

Your hormones also start to change quickly after birth, so, at this point, you're on an emotional roller coaster. Not only are the hormones changing your typical demeanor, but you are also sleep deprived, which can cause things to escalate. For me, I was feeling a mix of joy with a new baby, body frustration that I was not as mobile as before with the surgery, nervousness about being able to breastfeed, and exhaustion. I felt pressure from family and friends to message them as much as they were messaging me, but I also felt so much love from family and friends from their support. I felt awe for my partner watching his transition to fatherhood but also frustration in my partner because he could not read my mind. My feelings were truly all over the place and very conflicting.

On day five, my incredibly supportive parents and sister were coming over to meet Harper for the first time, and they wanted to bring dinner. Nice, right? They asked me what I wanted them to pick up, and I gave them three options for takeout. My mom didn't want any of the options I presented. I burst into tears because I could not emotionally handle the pressure of finding more restaurants to make them happy, the guilt of them picking up dinner for me, and then hosting them at my house while trying to keep on a newborn's schedule. I almost told them not to come, but my husband stepped in and figured it out, and we had a wonderful evening.

Let's unpack the above. In retrospect, having my family over is usually a very easy, low-pressure event. When you are a new mom, though, your mental load is already overcapacity with everything you must do for your baby, not to mention taking care of yourself and others in your household.

As we talked about before, your two most important priorities are 1) nurturing your baby and 2) healing your body and mind. The second priority, aka you, can get put on the back burner, and that is when breakdowns can happen.

In this case, I should have taken care of myself by telling my family that they needed to pick up whatever they wanted or delay coming over until I was in a better place mentally. It is okay to focus your time and effort on yourself postpartum. It is not selfish; it is essential for healing so that you can be the best mom you can be. I knew I needed to set better boundaries for myself but didn't listen to my inner voice when I was hitting my limit.

Society makes it seem like we should rebound immediately to our pre-momma selves but in reality, we don't. We have plenty of time to do what we need to do to heal before inviting other pressures into our environment.

Listen to your body and know your limits so you can express your needs—when and how you need them.

Working Out

When it comes to getting your body back into pre-baby shape, you may want to reframe your expectations for your body postpartum. Your body has gone through a major transformation and will never be the exact same as it was before. Postpartum is a time to reevaluate what makes you feel good in your body and reassess your goals for your physical health. Give yourself grace and the time to hit your goals.

Your body will need that time. You will likely still have a "bump" and look pregnant for a while after you deliver as your organs readjust. It can take up to six weeks for your uterus to shrink fully (WebMd,

2023).

If you decide to breastfeed, it will drastically improve your body's recovery time. Breastfeeding releases oxytocin, which can help the uterus contract faster. In addition to that, on average, breastfeeding burns an extra 500 calories a day, as you are making food for your little one (Cleveland Clinic, 2022). It is vital to nourish your body to keep up with its caloric demand and keep hydrated while pumping. Doing so will ensure that your milk supply is not affected. It is nice to eat whatever you want, guilt-free, through your breastfeeding journey and still shed some of your baby weight.

Even if you are not breastfeeding, you are still burning extra calories from carrying your adorable baby around all day. If you are surprised about how strong you start to feel after lifting and lugging your baby and all their accessories (bags, strollers, pack-and-plays, laundry bins, etc.), just wait until you see your stamina once your kiddo gets moving and you must chase them around!

Once you are able, taking walks is an excellent way to get your body moving. After my C-section, it took me two full weeks to gain enough strength to walk to the end of our driveway. It was a balance of not pushing myself too hard while getting a much-needed mental reprieve of being outside and taking steps toward my previously capable self.

Some of my most enjoyable memories of maternity leave were taking walks of varying lengths with Harper in the stroller bassinet. She often slept, but when she was awake, she loved looking at the tree branches overhead. Those walks and fresh air really helped my mental state and helped change up our daily routine. We also tried to take different routes every day to make the days slightly different as well and get a new perspective. If you're able, I highly recommend walking as a useful tool in your recovery journey.

Outside of the walks, one of my "time for me" activities incorporated into Harper's nap times was yoga and stretching. When you have a baby, you hunch over a lot. You are hunched over their bassinet, you hunch over them while feeding, you hunch over them while changing diapers, and breastfeeding, and cleaning, and cooking, and from exhaustion, and from all sorts of other things. With that and the additional five- to eight-pound weight of your peanut, who you carry around all the time, your shoulders can become very tense, and your body can become tight.

For me, yoga helped counteract the repetitive movements of newborn momming to open my chest and relax my neck. I found numerous postpartum yoga and stretching videos on YouTube that I did while Harper was on her play mat next to me or napping. Even if I stretched for just 5-10 minutes, I felt much more refreshed afterwards.

In addition to all that, regardless of how you birthed your child, you may also have Diastasis Recti. About two-thirds of women have Diastasis Recti, a condition where your abdominal muscles going down the middle of your stomach separate due to stretching while pregnant. That separation can cause your belly to bulge for years after birth if not corrected with core strengthening exercises. Diastasis does not hurt, but it does feel very odd. When you engage your core, it can feel like you have a one- to two-finger width wide gap running vertically down between your abs.

Your pelvic floor muscles may also have weakened or become too tight after having your baby. This may lead to leakage or incontinence after the baby. If you still experience pelvic pain, leakage, frequent urination, or fecal incontinence a few weeks after birth, make sure to talk to your doctor. They may recommend pelvic floor therapy or exercises to help strengthen or relax those muscles and get you back to normal.

With all that in mind, taking a slow and steady approach to yoga or stretching postpartum will do wonders for your tight muscles, help build your core, and help your mental well-being with real progress towards building your body confidence back.

I was very tempted to write "your pre-baby body back" there, but honestly, your body will never be the same as it was before the baby. What it can be is a new, physical representation of your best self as a momma. It can reflect the strength it took to grow, birth, and nurture another human. It can be the physical form of the appreciation you have for your body in this amazing journey.

Just think about how incredible your body is. For many of you reading this right now, you have a little baby growing inside you. Your womb is a safe place for that growing bundle of love, providing nutrients and protection from the outside world and the building blocks for such complex development. Your body naturally knows how to safely deliver that baby into the world. Your body knows how to heal you while making nutritionally complete food for your baby through your breasts. How complex and amazing is that!

Yet, society puts so much pressure on our bodies that are already working overtime to go immediately back to looking like we have not had a baby at all. If anything, I am proud of my C-section scar. I am proud of my once perky, but now slightly deflated, boobies that provided nine months of breast milk for Harper. I am thankful to my body for getting pregnant after two years of trying and then growing our little girl.

I have made a conscious effort to recognize the astounding beauty of the female body and just how incredible it is. I am giving my body the same grace I am giving my mind in alleviating the outside pressure so it can heal over the time it requires. I am nurturing it with the right foods, with walks, stretches, yoga, and sometimes cookie dough ice cream, and I know that it will respond with strength and endurance as my body and my mind progress through life together.

That is why I choose to say, "Building your body confidence back." It takes time to learn that appreciation and find that confidence, but by treating your body right and looking at what it has done and continues to do, that confidence will come.

Hair Loss

I literally thought I was going to go bald. I have thick hair and am used to seeing a good amount come out in the shower. A few weeks after I had Harper though, the amount of hair coming out in my hand as I lathered, washed, wrung out, and dried my hair gave me heart palpitations. I could have made a wig with all the hair I lost! The hair that was left on my head was brittle and stuck out from all different angles.

Ryan even said something about my "lost locks." My hair would attach to his shirts, get stuck in his toes, and get picked up on the bottom of his socks. Those socks worked better at picking up the hair than a heavy-duty Swiffer duster!

You may be walking around these days letting your thick, pregnancy hair whip in the wind like a shampoo model. With all those prenatal vitamins in your system, your increased blood circulation, and all the estrogen your body is making, your hair probably looks fabulous as it is growing faster and is not shedding as often. Your nails are also probably looking healthier and growing faster than usual. Please enjoy that while it lasts. There is a reason for the famous "mom bun" hairstyle.

Postpartum, you will start to see your hair fall out at potentially alarming rates between three and four months. With the changes in your hormones, you will start to shed all the hair that did not shed while you were pregnant. This shedding ramps up and usually peaks around four to five months postpartum. I was not too worried about it at first, but after a few months, every shower I took had more and more hair by the drain, and my hairbrush was filled with my beautiful strands.

Queue the mom-bun. Not only is the mom-bun the most convenient way to get your hair out of your face, but it also keeps the hair on your head instead of falling out on the floor around you. Not to mention, it is cute!

Don't worry, though. After your hair sheds, it will grow back. It does take time for the new hair to grow in, and it will have its awkward stage as it grows out. I had so many short hairs sticking out from all angles as they went from half an inch to an inch long, two inches, and then eventually long enough to clip back and then pull into my bun with all my other hair. The frizz is real, and hairspray and bobby pins are your best friends.

If your hair is medium to long, it can take a year or more for your hair to grow out to its previous length and thickness. Keeping up with your prenatal vitamins after pregnancy will help the growing process. When you start to see clumps in your drain, remind yourself that it will come back eventually. Give it time, just like the rest of your body!

CHAPTER FOUR
Sleep

Sleep is going to be hard to come by for a while. There is the old adage of "sleep when the baby sleeps," which makes me say, "Well duh, except...". The exception is that while your baby sleeps during the day, the timer starts to either get other tasks done or get some "you" time in. When you try to sleep at night, you may be wrestling with new-mom thoughts, have to get up to express your swollen "milk machines" at different timelines than your baby, or have trouble falling to sleep with all their little noises. All those interruptions detract from your amount of sleep, the duration of sleep, and sleep quality.

It is important to remember that this stage is temporary. You will get more sleep eventually. Each week that you progress will get easier, and the duration of sleep will get longer. Don't forget that!

In the early days, the lack of quality sleep may take a toll on your mental well-being. Even though I understood every sleep period would likely get disrupted, I found myself getting very disgruntled when my precious sleep time was shorter than anticipated or interrupted. The feelings I had when I woke up at those times were not my usual, positive self, and I knew I needed to reset my expectations.

What helped me cope was shifting how I viewed my day. Instead of approaching my day as a whole bunch of hours awake, followed by a whole bunch of hours asleep, I reset my day to a 24-hour clock with three-to-four-hour cycles. Some daytime hours that previously were awake hours were relabeled for sleep (with heavy duty blackout curtains, you can make any time feel like nighttime, right?). Some nighttime hours were now awake time. Since my expectations were reset, being awake from 3 to 4 AM when everyone else got to sleep didn't fill me with negativity. I knew my sleep hours would come later, and it eventually felt like a part of my 24-hour day.

Even if it is not actual sleep, general rest during daylight hours will give your body time to heal and your brain space decompress. If you find your brain wired because of new baby things, and you can't sleep at 10 AM but your baby is down for a nap, then consider reading or just lying with your eyes closed or meditating. Set yourself up for a potential snooze fest by wearing comfortable clothes, getting comfy with your favorite blanket or pillow, closing screens and their bright lights, and doing anything else that makes you feel relaxed.

Regardless of your approach to segmenting your day, there are a few tricks you can implement that could help you get tasks done quickly so that you get the rest you need when you have the opportunity.

Safe Spaces

Set up a few safe spaces for your baby around the house where you can put the baby down while awake or asleep. Ensure that these spaces are close to you so you can watch the baby while doing your tasks.

We had a portable, lightweight rocker with harness straps that was small enough to bring around the house with me. Harper liked the movement of the rocker, and we hung a few toys from the handle of the rocker above Harper to keep her entertained while I worked, showered, cooked, pumped, and more. I felt confident that she would be safely strapped into that rocker, just a glance away, while I was caring for myself, my partner, or our family!

We also had a bassinet in the living room so that Harper could wiggle or sleep by us while we watched TV. We could easily check on her, and being in the living room had the added benefit of Harper getting used to other noises while she slept. With two dogs in the house, there was always something making noise. We kept making our usual level of noise around Harper, even when sleeping, and she has turned out to be a very sound sleeper!

While some consistent background noise is okay, random, startling noises are not. Put a note on your front door letting delivery people or visitors know that there is a newborn. Asking them to gently knock instead of ringing the doorbell, especially if you have dogs that will bark at strangers or the bell, will be a nap-saver!

You can also try to schedule sleep times around when neighbors mow or blow their lawns or bang around their apartment. Asking your neighbors to avoid loud noises at certain times is perfectly reasonable as well. While you can't prevent all noises, it never hurts to ask or plan ahead!

Baby Wearing

Wearing your baby while you do tasks is very freeing. You can wear them while they are awake or asleep! You get multiple benefits with babywearing. There are the physical benefits of skin-to-skin bonding with your baby and the fact that wearing that extra weight around the house is a mini workout and burns more calories. Your baby is also in a safe, soothing place while you get two free arms to use for other things. From carriers to wraps to t-shirts with baby pockets, there are so many options to create a comfortable baby wearing experience for you and your baby. By wearing your baby, you can knock tasks off the list faster and set aside extra time to relax and rest yourself.

Partner Support

For those raising your little one with a partner, ask your partner to give you the time you need to rest. They do not always know when you are exhausted and cannot always tell when you need a break. Regardless of if that break is just fifteen minutes to a few hours, ask for what you need and set your boundaries so that your time is impactful.

I tend to say things like, "Wake me if you need anything," when my actual need is not to be disturbed so that I can get the deep rest my body or mind requires. Ryan is very capable of looking after Harper without me. Giving him the option for support during his watch does not help him gain confidence in his solo parenting abilities through problem solving. Setting the right boundaries for my rest would have made that time more fruitful for us both. Be vocal about your needs and ask for some interruption-free sleep time when you need it.

Family Support

You know all those people commenting on your baby's picture on Facebook, telling you how cute your munchkin is? Ask some of them to visit so you can nap. You do not need to be entertaining during this time. Hand your cute one over to your friends or family while you go hit the hay.

Sleeping at Night

If you are reading this while currently in the third trimester, you are probably already getting practice waking up multiple times in the middle of the night to pee. Your body is training you for the wake-up routine to come, or at least, that is how it seemed for me. While pregnant, restless leg syndrome made it hard for me to fall asleep and, with Harper using my bladder as a trampoline, I woke up every few hours to use the loo. Once Harper came, the sleep interruptions were about the same in frequency, but my nightly awake time increased from just a few minutes to 30 to 60 minutes.

Do you know what the hardest part of the postpartum nightly routine was for me? Getting out of my nice warm, cozy bed. If I could manage the mental strength to get up, I could handle the rest of it with relative, sleep deprived, ease. So can you.

Alternatively, some moms may find it more difficult to fall asleep. Around 60% of women   experience insomnia, difficulty getting to sleep, maintaining sleep, and getting quality sleep from late pregnancy through eight weeks postpartum (Swanson, L. M., et al, 2020). Changes in your sleep schedule, fluctuating hormone levels , postpartum depression, anxiety or fear, baby wakeups, night sweats, and all the other new mom "perks" can contribute to sleep disruption and insomnia (Ruscio, D., 2022).

Women with poor sleep quality are 3.3 times more likely to have postpartum depression (Iranpour, et al, 2016), so it is incredibly important to take steps to encourage rest. A few thought starters are below:

- **Have a bedtime routine.** Routines are beneficial for both kids and adults. They help you relax and signal to your body that it is time for sleep. We will go into the bed-time schedule a little later, but establishing your routine for bed is important too.

- **Set the mood for sleep 15 to 20 minutes before bed.** Dim your lights, pull the black-out curtains, have a warm shower, snuggle up in your most comfy PJ's, cuddle up to your favorite pillow, enjoy a sleepy-time tea, make sure your room is at the right temperature, and set the environment you need to feel relaxed.

- **Put the screens away.** The light from screens can suppress melatonin production . Melatonin is a hormone secreted after dark that helps you fall asleep (Cooper, J. A.). Studies indicate that melatonin levels fluctuate postpartum, so further disruption from screen time can make it harder to fall asleep (Ruscio, D., 2022). It is important to note that screen light can have the same impact on your baby's ability to fall asleep. Limiting exposure to bright lights from your phone, TV, or other devices before bedtime will help you both. Setting a "bedtime" for your phone will help with light exposure and prevent accidental late nights from mindless scrolling. Use those apps on your phone to keep you awake at 2 AM while nursing or pumping, not right before closing your eyes to sleep.

- **Meditation is another tool for winding down before sleep.** Slowing your mind's activity, focusing on your breath, and reducing your stress through meditation have been proven to improve sleep quality. Regular meditation, even for just a few minutes, can improve your overall mood and mindset as well. If you don't know where to start, there are thousands of apps and YouTube videos for meditation beginners!

- **Exercise.** Regular exercise is proven to improve sleep onset and sleep quality . Exercise can help ease postpartum anxiety and other depressive symptoms that also impact sleep (Singh, A., and Pacheco, D., 2023). While it may be slow going at first, a 30-minute walk around the neighborhood, yoga, or any other form of moderate movement to get your heart rate up will go a long way.

In addition to that, you need to build your sleep confidence with your baby at night. Babies make many strange noises that you would not expect throughout the night. It will take time to get used to them, learn what they mean for your baby, and become confident that your baby will wake you up when they need you. That confidence will help you sleep more soundly at night.

SIDS

On top of the stress of strange noises comes the anxiety caused by sudden infant death syndrome, also known as SIDS. SIDS is when an otherwise healthy baby unexpectedly dies during the night. Most often, it happens when the baby cannot rouse itself from sleep or turn over and lacks oxygen or breathes in too much carbon monoxide. Causes for SIDS can be linked to low birth weights, respiratory issues, birth defects that impact the brain and the baby's ability to rouse from sleep, unsafe sleeping conditions, or sleeping on the tummy instead of the back (Mayo Clinic, Postpartum care, 2022).

SIDS is a terrifying concept for any new parent and can invoke anxiety and prevent you from sleeping well. The good news is SIDS is rare, and you can drastically reduce the risk of SIDS in a few easy ways:

- **Providing a safe sleeping environment.** Have your baby sleep in your room in a crib, bassinet, or bed specifically designed for babies. While it may be tempting to fall asleep with your baby in your bed, co-sleeping at an early age can be very dangerous. Adult beds can be too soft, and the baby can suffocate if they get in between the wall and mattress or bed frame or under a pillow. Additionally, an adult can roll over in the middle of the night and cover the baby's face or crush them accidentally. While some parents opt to co-sleep, be aware of all the risks and make the safest decision for you and your baby.

- **What goes in the crib.** This includes having a firm mattress and removing all blankets, pillows, bumpers, and toys from the crib. There are also swaddles with zippers and Velcro to make them more secure at night instead of blankets. You can find more resources on building a safe sleep environment online or through your doctor.

- **Sleep position.** Having your baby sleep on their back so that their face is up towards the ceiling instead of face down on their belly or their side. Remember, babies this young cannot turn over, hold their heads up, push themselves up, or move out of uncomfortable or dangerous positions. Your job is to make sure they do not get into those positions to begin with.

- **Breastfeeding.** Studies show that breastfed babies have a lower likelihood of SIDS.

- **Temperature control.** Ensure that your baby does not get overheated. Babies cannot sweat or self-regulate their temperature, so you will need to help regulate their temperature by how few or how many layers they wear. Monitor the room's temperature and ensure they are dressed and swaddled accordingly. There are plenty of online resources to show you how many layers of clothes your baby needs at different temperatures.

- **Educate your friends and family on safe sleep procedures.** Do not assume your loved ones and caregivers will know how to make a safe sleep environment. If your baby is sleeping over at grandma and grandpa's house or napping at auntie and uncle's place, walk them through safe sleep rules to ensure everyone is on the same page.

If you implement safe sleep practices, you and your baby will be set up for success. When the fear of SIDS creeps into your mind at night, remember that SIDS is rare and go through the list of everything you've done to create the best environment for your baby. Your sleep confidence will grow over time.

Bedtime Routine

It will take a few days, weeks, or months to get your new nighttime routine down. From figuring out your baby's schedule with sleep and food and your schedule for your changing body, it might be tough. Your bedside table will now be filled with burp cloths, bottles, nipple shields, milk catchers, pump parts, snot suckers, water bottles, and more. You'll need to math your way to figuring out your and your baby's bedtime and set your alarm to wake you and baby up two and a half to three hours for diaper changes and feeding. After your baby goes down for the night, you will likely need to pump or prepare your formula bottles for the evening in advance. There is much to think about with an already exhausted brain, and your mental load may feel high.

Don't be afraid to go to bed early. As I mentioned earlier, I love to sleep. The few weeks after giving birth were exhausting for me, so I set my "in-bed" time for nine PM. Our schedule looked like this for the most part:

- 6-6:30 PM: Harper bedtime
- 8-8:30 PM: Night feed #1
- 8:30-9 PM: Pump and wind down for bed
- 9-9:30 PM: If we had energy, Ryan and I would read for a little while and have lights out by 9:30 PM.
- 10:30-11 PM: Night feed #2
- 1-1:30 AM: Night feed #3
- 3:30-4 AM: Night feed #4
- 4:01 AM: Ryan would take over duties, and I would get my four-hour long stretch of sleep until 8 AM.

You might ask why I only got a four-hour stint as my "long sleep". While Ryan could take care of Harper with a bottle, he could not help with my boobs. If you do not consistently express yourself or breast-feed on the right hour schedule, your boobs will get hard and tender and they will wake you up. I craved more sleep, but the consequences were hilariously dire. The few times when my alarm failed to go off and I slept in, my breasts felt like they would explode! They started leaking as soon as I got out of bed and I had to sprint into the kitchen to get my pump supplies and back track with a paper towel to clean up the drip path on the floor. Keep in mind that you will be up every few hours for your baby or your body.

I relied on my alarm clock as back up if my body didn't wake me up on time and Harper didn't cry out for food. At first, I used the audio alarm on my phone at night. It was startlingly loud enough to wake me up, but it also woke Ryan as well. Ryan discovered that my watch had a vibration alarm function which was strong enough to wake me gently while not waking Ryan. It was a game changer! If you do not need a super loud, annoying alarm to wake you, and have another person sharing your bed, the vibration watch alarms are a great alternative to help improve both of your sleep quality and keep you on schedule.

Outside of smartwatches, you will likely need to wear some other new things to bed. You will need your sexy adult diapers (girl, you can make anything look good, just own it!) you will want to wear nursing bras or tanks as well. This will make your night duties more convenient and soak up any leakage.

I tried the pumping and nursing bras but found that nursing tanks worked way better for me. Pumping bras have slits over your nipples for easy access, but those slits can chafe and cause nipple irritation. Also, nursing bras required an additional shirt to go on top. I lived in nursing tanks 24/7 for nine months while pumping and found that throwing on cozy jackets or shawls with front openings was much more coinvent than taking shirts on and off whenever I needed to feed Harper.

Those tanks also soaked up all my sweat. Since estrogen and pro-gesterone levels drop so much postpartum, you will likely experience night sweats like never before. Breastfeeding can also exacerbate sweating as those hormones stay at lower levels (Cleveland Clinic, 2022). I would wake up so drenched that I had to sleep in a towel sandwich, a towel on top and another below me, to soak it all up. Night sweats usually peak around two weeks after giving birth and last until week six. They are just another reason to keep as hydrated as possible with water and hydration replenishment drinks throughout your postpartum experience.

Also, for all you stomach sleepers who are excited to sleep on your tummy post-baby belly, if you are breastfeeding, you will not be able to sleep on your front until after you're done breastfeeding. Your boobs will be too sensitive for that, and you might super-soak your bed!

Pillow Talk

If you have a partner, talk to them about night shifts. Some new moms may choose to get night nurses, but for those of us who cannot do that, it is important to set the right expectations with your partner so that you have the sleep support you need.

As I mentioned, Ryan took the shift with Harper after four AM. He would handle all crying, diapers, feedings, and anything else that came up while I got my precious four-hour stretch. I would wake up to Harper crying at 4:05 AM and be so relieved that I could count on Ryan to take over. Our shared responsibilities helped me get more, higher quality sleep.

I did feel guilty that he had to get up early and take care of Harper. I also had the urge to help him. But I didn't. I slept. I had done the same tasks multiple times already while he slept. He could handle his portion of the responsibility. My time was better spent resting rather than assisting him when he was perfectly capable of tending to Harper's needs.

We had a conversation early on to set our bedtime rules. Having concrete responsibilities helped us get more sleep and helped prevent miscommunications, fights, or resentment from assuming someone was going to do something that they didn't or when one partner wasn't holding up their end of the bargain. There are many things you will have to do for your baby that your partner cannot, so guiding them on where they can help you is essential for divvying up shared duties.

Another conversation that you should have with your partner is about how long you will have your baby sleep in your room. This is a very personal decision completely based on comfort level. We had Harper in our bedroom for the first month that she was home. Having her inches from me at night gave me immense security that she was OK and that all her crazy noises were just funny, natural, and not scary.

After we built confidence and were comfortable with our routine and Harper's noises, we realized that those noises frequently woke both of us up throughout the night. We also learned that Harper would let us know when she needed something by crying and waking up. Her cries could easily be heard over our monitor with video. At four weeks, we made the decision to move her into her bedroom across the hall so that we could sleep deeper for the limited time we were asleep. While that was difficult at first, it had an immensely positive impact on our energy levels, mental health, and relationship throughout the day.

CHAPTER FIVE

Nourishment

I have always been flat-ish-chested. During pregnancy, though, my boobs ballooned up and, boy, was I proud of "my girls"! I flaunted them in outfits, and they were one of the few perky and exciting physical changes of pregnancy for me. You may have a different opinion about yours going into your postpartum journey. Whatever your opinion is though, if this is your first kid, I have a feeling that your relationship with your "girls" to date has been more about how they look versus what they can do. If there is one thing I gained postpartum, it was a new appreciation for my tatas and respect for their amazing abilities.

Even before you deliver, your boobs are getting ready for their new job. A few weeks before the baby comes, you may have some colostrum leakage and feel tenderness, swelling, or sensitivity. After your baby has arrived, your milk "comes in" and it is time to decide if you want to breastfeed, pump, do a combo of both, or dry up your supply and go with formula.

Remember, your number one priority is nurturing your baby which can be done through all three feeding methods. As long as your baby is eating, you are doing what is right for them, so don't let any outside pressure or opinions (outside of your medical professional for a medically necessary reason) make you feel differently or that you are less than a good mom. As the saying goes, a fed baby is a happy baby.

Breastfeeding

There is a reason your nipple looks like a giant target on your breast. Your baby's instinct is to find your nipple and suckle for food. When babies are born, they can only see eight to ten inches away, so that target lets them know they are close to their next meal. You may have already seen funny videos on social media of babies trying to suck on their mom's faces, dad's chests, or other objects they mistake for their mom's breasts!

Not only is breastfeeding good for baby, but it has health benefits for mom! According to the CDC, mothers who breastfeed have a reduced risk of breast and ovarian cancer, type 2 diabetes, and high blood pressure (CDC, 2023). Additionally, breastfeeding produces increased levels of oxytocin, which can help reduce anxiety and depressive symptoms (Stuebe, A. M., Grewen, K., & Meltzer-Brody, S., 2013).

Breastfeeding can trigger many emotions. Latching, biting, nipple trauma, production, and not knowing how much your baby is eating can all be frustrating, painful, and energy-draining. Many feeding sessions are at 1, 2, 3, 4 AM after you're woken by baby cries and are just trying to stay awake while your baby eats. Being the sole provider of food for your baby can also be overwhelming, especially if you have production or latching issues. However, for me and many other women, it is a truly beautiful experience.

Breastfeeding is a bond between you and your baby that no one else in the world will ever have. If you choose to exclusively breastfeed, your body is providing your baby with everything they need to grow and develop. Not only that, but feeding time is a sacred time between only the two of you. It enables skin-to-skin bonding as your baby clings to you because they need you and the nourishment you create for them. It is also a time for you both to feel each other's warmth and build that wonderful feeling of love.

Remembering those moments with Harper has me tearing up as I write this. Yes, I did spend a ton of that time scrolling through social media or watching TV trying to stay awake during feeds. Yes, I do remember her crying in public while I was trying to get undressed enough to get her on my breast as quickly as possible while not flashing everyone looking at us from the commotion. Yes, I did get frustrated trying to use a nipple shield so she could latch or trying to understand why she was fussy after she was done. Yes, I did get jealous that Ryan got to sleep through the night since I was the only one with the feeding ability for a while. Yes, sometimes I did need space from Harper because her constant need for my body was a lot to process. But those things are not what I vividly remember. My main memories of that time are looking down at Harper, smiling, while admiring her little face and loving our cuddle time while it lasted.

No matter how long or how short your breastfeeding journey is, soak it in, try to remember it, and be reminded of how incredible your body is. It did just grow a human and now it is sustaining both of you for as long as you need it to do so.

Lactation

Newborns are ravenous little creatures and, as you will soon find out, they want to eat every two and a half to three hours (sometimes more or sometimes less). Breastmilk production is a supply-and-demand game so, the more your baby eats or the more you pump, the more you will produce. Because of this, you will be on the clock, but not just your baby's clock. You will know when it is time to feed as you will feel your milk "come in".

Your milk's arrival feels like a rush of swelling that comes on the outer sides of your breasts and is followed by a feeling of fullness. It is not painful, but you know when it happens. Time is not the only thing that triggers lactation though. Hearing your baby's cries, thinking about your baby, and even skin-to-skin time can trigger the release of hormones that let your body know it is time to feed and can cause your breasts to fill and even leak. It is remarkable that your body naturally creates the food your baby needs on demand!

Speaking of your milk, did you know that there are different types?

I already mentioned the colostrum which is the nutrient-dense milk that comes right before and after your baby is born. Colostrum is a richer color and is thicker than the milk that follows. It also contains many antibodies to help build your baby's immune system and protect them from viral bacteria and infections (Cleveland Clinic, 2022). Speaking of, research suggests that your nipples absorb the saliva from your baby and then your mammary glands change your milk to adjust to your baby's needs from the makeup of that saliva (Newmark, L., M., 2022). If your baby is sick, your breasts can formulate milk with the antibodies needed to help them fight infection! Amazing, huh?

After two to four days of colostrum, transitional milk starts to flow. This milk is less dense but higher in fat and calories than colostrum.

The last phase is the mature milk which will be what your body makes for the rest of your breastfeeding journey. Mature milk is 90%

water to help your baby keep hydrated. The remaining 10% is all the nutrients needed for your baby to thrive.

Mature milk also has two stages: the foremilk and the hindmilk. The foremilk comes out when you first start to feed, is mostly water, and is filled with vitamins and protein. The hindmilk is what makes the baby fuller as it is thicker with fat and the needed sustenance for weight gain. If you pump your milk or express it into bottles, you can see the differences pretty clearly!

One added benefit of breast milk is that it changes the way your baby's poop smells! With Harper, her poop often smelled like movie theater-grade, buttered popcorn. I never thought I would consider my daughter's poop to smell good or to make us want to have a movie night! It was the strangest thing, but we preferred that smell to the very stinky alternative of formula or solid food poop. Buttered popcorn is a frequent smell, but other parents have reported other sweet smells like oatmeal and cupcakes.

Something to keep in mind is that everyone's body produces different volumes of milk. It is important to know going into your postpartum journey that your milk production may vary and there may be some work involved to increase your supply to keep up with baby's demand. Not being able to create enough milk does not mean that you are a bad mom. It just means you will have to put in some extra time and effort. Remember, a fed baby is a happy baby, regardless of where the food comes from. If you are feeding your baby, you are doing your job!

With that said, there are a few ways to help set you up for success with milk production:

- Feed or pump until your breasts are fully drained. The

demand will create supply.

- Feed and pump consistently (Eight to ten times a day).

- Keep very hydrated.

- Make sure to eat enough calories. Breastfeeding can burn between 500-700 calories a day. In order to make the food your baby needs, you need to get enough food too!

If you continue to have low supply, your lactation consultant or medical professional will be able to provide more guidance on building your breastfeeding output. If your supply is not fully meeting your baby's needs and you want to continue using breast milk instead of moving to formula, there are breast milk banks with donated breast milk or breast milk for purchase that can help support your feeding goals.

Your milk supply should start to regulate after about six to twelve weeks of breastfeeding as your body gets used to the demands of your baby. You may find that your breasts do not get quite as swollen or uncomfortable, you can go a little longer without feeding before feeling discomfort, and you may leak less often. You may be able to start pushing for a little longer sleep without dropping the overall amount of milk you produce.

You may overproduce breast milk. Hyperlactation is when you yield more breast milk than your baby needs. This can be a good thing if you are also pumping and want to have a breast milk storage built up after you discontinue pumping and breastfeeding. It can also make it difficult for your baby to latch or for you to manage additional leakage from the oversupply and cause additional breast discomfort (van Veldhuizen-Staas, C. G. A. 2007).

Don't be surprised if one of your breasts outperforms the other in milk supply. My right breast was the production champion; always giving an ounce or two more than my left. I was a little judge-y and disappointed with the left boob for a while, giving more credit to my right, but then my right breast decided to unleash the floodgates.

When Harper cried, my Righty would spring a leak! When I tried to use it to feed Harper, the milk came so quickly that it literally waterboarded, or milk-boarded, Harper! She couldn't keep up with how quickly the milk came out of my nipple and it was too much for her. Leftie was much slower and had a better flow for Harper to feed from. I ended up adapting my approach by breastfeeding on the left while pumping the right. If I didn't want to pump, I used a milk catcher (a suction cup for your breast that catches leakage) so that I could reuse any extra milk.

Hyperlactation can cause issues with feeding as babies can choke or not latch. If Hyperlactation becomes an issue for you, there are special breastfeeding positions (also known as holds) to help slow the flow and make it easier on both you and baby.

Overall, no matter what your supply situation is, there is a learning curve to your body, its rhythm, and how much it will produce. Be patient with your body, go with the flow, and make sure to nourish yourself. Your body knows what it needs to do for both you and your baby. If you still have concerns, lactation consultants or your doctor are great resources for helping you along the way.

I babysat my neighbor's two sons growing up. Our families grew close and kept in touch over the years. As it turns out, Dawn, the mom, was a lactation specialist! She was the one who gifted me the breast massagers I relied on so heavily. She was also an amazing resource while I was at home and having trouble with latching. I texted her at the wee hours of the night when I struggled with Harper in my arms.

She recommended different breastfeeding positions and various nipple creams to soothe my aching and cracked nipples. Her advice and kindness replaced my doubts with confidence.

Most hospitals and insurance providers cover lactation support after birth, even after leaving the hospital or birthing centers. In addition to that, there are free lactation hotlines, lactation support groups, and other free services that help moms in need. If you are struggling, don't hesitate to look up the resources available to you so that you can get the help you need.

Breastfeeding also has other effects on your body. For example, most breastfeeding mommas will not get their period back until after they stop breastfeeding because hormones like prolactin, which helps your body produce milk, can stop ovulation. I pumped and breastfed for eight months and did not get my period for another three months after I dried up!

Note, it is a common misconception that, since you have not had your period, you cannot get pregnant while breastfeeding. That is not true. There are a lot of women that have been "surprised" only a few months after having their baby that they had another on the way. Make sure to always use protection with your partner postpartum until you are ready to add to your family. Most doctors will recommend waiting a year before trying again so that your body can heal properly before conceiving.

Speaking of sexy time, the hormones after delivery and during breastfeeding reduce the body's production of natural lubricant, meaning you can feel very dry down there. Sex can also be painful as your body is healing. Most medical professionals will recommend that you wait four to six weeks (especially if you had a C-section or vaginal tear) to properly heal. To set you and your partner up for success, make sure to talk to your partner about your body and how you feel beforehand. Set the right expectations around taking it slow, communicating if you need to stop or need more time, and using protection. Invest in the right products to make sure you have an enjoyable experience and take the right precautions for family planning.

Mastitis

The longer you wait between breastfeeding sessions, the fuller your breasts will feel and the more likely they are to start to drip or leak. This is why most breastfeeding and pumping bras and tanks have padding that soaks up leakage. Eventually, your breasts will become uncomfortable, tender, and harder as they get fuller. They may even hurt.

This can be especially true in the mornings after you get a longer run of sleep. I remember waking up some mornings because my boobs were rock hard and lumpy, and felt like they would explode. If Harper was still asleep or had already eaten, I would have to run (not exaggerating) to the kitchen to grab my pump parts and relieve myself. It was intense but also very comical.

Letting your boobs fill up too much is not recommended for good reason. Milk buildup can lead to clogged ducts and mastitis. Mastitis is the inflammation of the mammary glands within the breast caused by infection from either clogged milk ducts or bacteria from your baby's mouth or your skin's surface entering your breast (Mayo Clinic, Postpartum care, 2022). You may have mastitis if you feel a tender lump in your breast where a clog is or see a red splotch on your breast. Mastitis can be very uncomfortable, and symptoms can include a high fever, chills, night sweats, breast pain, or tenderness.

While I tried my best to keep my girls in good shape, I got mastitis three times. It was awful. I got shivers that were so bad I could not physically hold Harper. I was so cold that I crawled in bed with multiple layers of clothing, a sheet, blanket, comforter, weighted blanket, and fluffy blanket on top of me (yes, that is six blanket layers) and was still freezing and shaking. After virtual doctor appointments that prescribed me antibiotics, multiple naps, and Tylenol that took my 103 fever down, I got through it each time. Trust me, it was not fun. Not to mention that Ryan had to take care of Harper while I was incapacitated. After those experiences, I used breast massagers with a warming function frequently to break up any blockages and pumped often.

Your main takeaway here is that prevention is key. The following can help prevent mastitis:

- Make sure to drain your breasts all the way when breastfeeding (or pumping) by draining one and then switching to the next.
- Try different breastfeeding positions with your baby for a full feed.
- Take care of your nipples with nipple cream to help with cracking or chafing.
- Make sure your baby latches properly.
- If you are pumping, be sure to use the right flange size. A flange size that is too big or too small can damage your nipple and be very painful (Unfortunately, I know from experience).

If you think you have mastitis, especially if you have a fever, call your doctor as soon as you can to ensure you can get back to health quickly.

Outside of some of the inconveniences of breastfeeding, overall, it is a very beautiful experience. Your body is literally making everything your baby needs to thrive as they grow into this world. It can be funny, frustrating, messy, and painful, but it is a bond unlike any other. Don't take that for granted.

I didn't know that Harper's "last latch" was going to be the end of that time in our life together. After that session, she rejected my breast for the bottle. It was the end of a beautiful era for me, and I did grieve the end afterward. Some of you may be ready for it to end and even celebrate that milestone, which is also great! Either way, try to remember this time, because it goes fast, and it is special.

Pumping

Women decide to pump their breast milk for many reasons. Some women do not like the act or feeling of breastfeeding, have had trauma which makes breastfeeding difficult for them, their babies do not latch, they want the convenience of having "milk on the go", they have supply issues and use pumping to supplement breastfeeding, they return to work and leave their baby in someone else's feeding care, the list goes on.

No matter the reason, pumping is a wonderful alternative to breastfeeding. Your baby will still get all the amazing nutrients of breast milk as they grow and develop while you get more flexibility.

Unlike your baby's set feeding schedule, you can start to have longer time frames between pumping sessions, increasing the flexibility in your schedule. Since feeding at night will take less time with a bottle and you can go longer between night pumps, you may potentially get longer periods of sleep once your milk production normalizes. You can give your partner more responsibility in the feeding journey as well since they can prepare and give the bottles to your baby just like you would. Bottles also allow you to track how much your baby is eating since the bottles have exact measurements.

Since Harper had trouble latching at first, I pumped to ensure she always had enough to be full between the two feeding methods. Ryan also took the morning shift with Harper. Having bottles of breast milk available for him to heat up and feed to Harper while I slept in the morning was a lifesaver.

Once I got into the pumping routine, I also found out I had an oversupply, so I froze my excess milk. That excess allowed me to give Harper breast milk for a full three months after I stopped my milk supply. In addition to that, my breastfeeding journey was during the 2022 formula shortage. Covid pandemic-related supply chain issues in 2021 created an initial shortage in baby formula in the US. In February of 2022, there was a voluntary recall contaminated formula from one of the largest manufactures in the US. That manufacturer also shut down one of their manufacturing facilities. Those events led to a formula scarcity and a surge in formula buying as people stockpiled for their needs. Out-of-stock rates for formula surpassed 74% nationally and over 90% in some states (Kalaitzandonakes, M., Ellison, B., and Coppess, J., 2023). Luckily, I was able to donate some of my milk to new mommas that were stressed about finding formula or nourishment for their babies and had trouble with their own supply. Helping those women and alleviating some of their worries during such a stressful time was incredibly rewarding for me.

Much of your first few weeks at home are spent trying to figure out your new schedule. Pumping and breastfeeding are massive parts of that schedule. I tried so many styles, cadences, positions, and timing before getting our routine down. You can pump one breast while breastfeeding from the other, you can breastfeed and then pump any remaining milk afterward. You can bottle feed and then pump on your own schedule.

Regardless of how you do it, you will need to pump every two and a half to three hours (eight to ten times a day) at first and then can adjust time and cadence after your milk regulates, but that also depends on your breastfeeding schedule. As mentioned, milk regulation happens about six to twelve weeks after you have your baby and is when the amount of milk you produce is no longer influenced as much by your hormones but really the amount you pump or that your baby takes in while feeding. Once your milk is established, your breast will not feel as full or firm before you express, you probably won't spring a leak as often, and you also may see a drop in your overall supply.

Overall, it can be a little overwhelming.

You will need to be OK with trial and error. You will find what works best for you over time. Again, as long as your baby is fed, the details of how are not as important. What will help is finding ways to alleviate your mental load of remembering everything. "Mom-brain" is real and having apps or reminders to help you remember everything will help alleviate your stress levels drastically.

I highly recommend downloading one of the many free apps available to track the needs of both you and your baby. From breastfeeding time, pumping time, pumping amount, feeding amount, diaper changes, more information about the contents of those diapers than you ever thought would need to be tracked, sleep and nap schedules, and more, those apps will help you keep on schedule and grow your new-mom confidence.

Additionally, I asked Siri or my Google Home to set reminders and alarms for me. If I pumped every three hours, I would ask Siri to set the alarm for three hours immediately after I pumped so I wouldn't have to remember when the time came again. Those alarms kept us on track with timing as well.

Breast Pumpies

Outside of figuring out your schedule, you will also need to test what breast pump is right for you and all the accessories. While pumps can seem straightforward, if you do not have the right flange sizes, they can damage your nipple, causing irritation and pain.

Flanges are the large cone-like pieces that cover your nipple. They have a small tube that your nipple moves in and out of. If that tube is too big or too small for you, it can cause issues. I didn't realize my pump came with two different flange sizes, so I was using both interchangeably depending on which one was clean at the time. One size was too big and caused swelling and a lot of pain. It took a few days and a lot of nipple cream for me to identify that the flanges were the problem. Of course, you cannot stop pumping and feeding while you are in pain or healing, so prevention is key to avoiding that situation altogether.

At the hospital, you will have the luxury of using the medical grade pumps and lactation consultants to show how. You can bring your at-home pump to the hospital, and the staff will confirm your flange size and ensure you know how long to pump, what settings to use, and how to clean your numerous pump parts correctly. The medical grade pump will have different instructions than the at-home kind, so make sure you ask about your specific type.

I used a cordless pump, meaning it did not need to be plugged into the wall while pumping. It had a night light on it for late-night pumps and a timer to automatically stop pumping after a set time. It also had multiple settings for the cadence and suction.

There are different settings on pumps that mimic the baby's nursing rhythms and encourage milk let-downs. At the start of feeding, the baby has short, shallow pulls, which tells your body it is time to produce milk. Once the milk starts to flow, your baby will switch to longer, deeper pulls to help draw out the milk. Your baby will use both feeding styles throughout a session, and most breast pumps have settings to mimic that as well.

While the pump was "cord-free", it had two long, dangling tubes that connected the pump to the flanges. Those tubes got caught on every drawer handle, doorknob, and stove knob while I tried to do things around the house. I almost melted the tubes a few times while trying to cook at the same time.

The tubes also got tangled on Harper frequently when I tried to simultaneously pump and feed. When that happened, the flange would get pulled off my breast or the tube out of the pump, and I would lose suction and leak, spilling the bottle or bag I was filling. The phrase "don't cry over spilled milk" does NOT apply to breast milk. You work hard for every ounce, and spilling any can be mentally taxing!

It was also tough to pick Harper up or carry her while pumping and lugging the pump around. After 6 months of dealing with the machine, I lost my patience with pumping altogether.

Seeing all my frustration with the pump, my husband surprised me with a pair of wearable breast pumps. Wearable pumps have small motors that go on top of individual milk catchers for each breast and can be worn under your clothing. They are truly cord and tube free! They were a game changer for me and extended my pumping journey by months.

I could do so much more while pumping. Cooking, cleaning, driving, and even pumping discreetly in the office on a work trip and on the airplane traveling for that trip, those pumps made it much more possible. They also collected just as much milk as my other traditional pump and were much quieter than my other pump.

Ultimately, I learned that the fewer cords, tubes, and inconveniences I had to maneuver around, the longer I could keep up with my pumping journey. While it may be more expensive upfront to invest in the right pump for you, if it extends the amount of time you pump, it will save you money on formula over time and a lot of stress as well.

Your Milk Bank

Milk management is probably not something you think or talk about when you decide to pump, but once you start pumping, it becomes a time-intensive job. After each pumping session, you will need to measure out your milk and store it in either bottles or bags. The amount of milk you portion out will depend on how much your baby is actively drinking.

In addition to that, the pressure of not spilling a single, tiny, itsy, drop of that precious milk you just worked so hard to make can cause stress.

Let me tell you now, you will spill milk and you may very well cry about that spilled milk. I know I did. We tipped entire bottles over accidentally. My pump bottle came loose and detached from the pump while it was pumping, spilling all over the floor. I didn't attach bags correctly to my flanges at two AM, so instead of having the milk go into the bag, it went all over the blanket and couch next to me. I didn't notice that until the end of my pump and my couch was soaked and smelled weird. The list of spills goes on.

How did I let all those spills happen, you ask? Well, a mix of exhaustion, lack of light during night pumps, exhaustion, baby distractions, and clumsiness due to exhaustion, will do that to you. Did I mention I was exhausted?

When the spills happen, and you start beating yourself up about it, remember to take your negative self-talk out with the trash and give yourself some grace. Accidents are, obviously, accidental. It will be okay. You will make more, and you have other options for food if you need them. You are still a good mom, and I will repeat, it is perfectly OK to cry about spilled milk.

Once you have successfully measured your milk into either the bags or bottles, you will need to decide how to store them. If you are making enough to keep up with your baby's needs, you may opt to put them in the fridge. If you produce more than your baby needs, you may freeze it. For both methods, there are some timeframes to consider:

- Freshly pumped milk can sit out at room temperature (below 77 degrees) for up to four hours (Mayo Clinic, Breast Milk Storage, 2022).
- Refrigerated breast milk needs to be used within four days, but three is typically recommended.
- Frozen breast milk is best used within three months of

freezing in a typical freezer. In a deep freezer, it can be stored for up to twelve months, but using it before six months is recommended.

There are specific freezer bags for milk storage that have measurements on them for easy use. Once I had a bag filled up, I laid it horizontally on a flat surface in my freezer (aka a Lean Cuisine box) so that it froze in a solid, flat block. I then stacked my individual bags in gallon-sized freezer bags and labeled each bag with the date range of milk for easy reference. That system helped me keep track of the order of bags that needed to be thawed and when.

Thawing milk is easy, but you have to do some math for how much you need in a day to know when and how much to thaw. A milk bag takes about 18 to 24 hours to thaw out in the fridge . Quick heating of the milk for a faster thaw through the microwave or on the stove is not recommended as it can break down important parts of the milk or not heat evenly (Mayo Clinic, Breast Milk Storage, 2022). If you need to speed up the thawing process, you can stick the bag in a bowl of warm water or run it under your sink's hot water instead.

Unlike your fresh milk, once frozen breast milk is completely thawed out, the milk needs to be used within 24 hours before it will go bad. You cannot refreeze it, either. Frozen milk can also smell different or sourer than fresh milk. The milk will also separate in the freezing process, so you may see the fattier, calorie-dense components get stuck on the bag while pouring. Make sure to shake the bag and blend the different milk components back in to get the milk's full benefit.

Once your baby's lips touch the fresh bottle, the "bottle usage" timer starts. When your baby starts to drink, the bacteria in their mouth are introduced to the milk, and those bacteria can grow over time. If the milk has been out too long, it can make your baby sick. The bottle must be used within the recommended hour of when they start drinking it, even if you put it in the fridge.

Milk storage and management can be a lot to keep track of. I highly recommend printing out the outline of recommended milk use timelines to alleviate your mental load.

Formula Feeding

Whether you decide to formula feed from birth or to transition to formula along the way, do not feel guilty about using formula. It is the second-best option to breast milk, and, for some parents, it is the only option. Again, as long as you are feeding your baby enough for them to grow big and strong, you are doing your job as a mom.

There are a lot of perks to formula feeding. For one thing, you do not have to worry about your boob's schedule in addition to your baby's schedule. You can lessen your responsibility load since your partner can prepare and feed your baby just as well as you can. You can be on the go as formula is easy to prepare and to travel with since it does not require refrigeration.

No matter when you decide to switch to formula or end your breastfeeding journey, you will have to stop your body's natural breast milk production process. The time it takes to stop your supply will depend on your levels of production at the time you decide to stop. For women who opt to formula feed from the start or have low supply, drying up can take a few days. For women with a decent supply or with oversupply like me, it could take a few weeks.

To "dry up", you will need to slowly increase the time between expressing your milk and gradually drop feeding or pumping sessions over time. In addition to that, you will not want to fully drain your breasts, but only drain enough to feel comfortable. You do not want to cause blockages in your milk ducts and potential mastitis by pushing yourself too long to let your breasts get too full. It can also be uncomfortable or painful to let yourself get too full. Ice packs help with swelling and some women even put cold cabbage leaves on their breasts to help with the discomfort and stop their supply sooner. Ultimately, it is up to you how fast or slow you want to go based on your body's abilities. You can always reach out to your doctor or lactation specialist for guidance along the way.

I referred to this process as "deflategate". My little boobies looked smashing all through pregnancy and breastfeeding. I was so excited about "my girls" and definitely flaunted them in outfits. They boosted my confidence when other parts of my body did not. After I stopped breastfeeding, though, they shrunk to a smaller size than pre-pregnancy and were nowhere near as perky.

During breastfeeding, your breasts are constantly increasing and decreasing in size. Like a balloon, if you constantly stretch and reduce the size, the shape does wear out and doesn't fill out the same way when mostly deflated.

While I do miss how they once looked, I am very proud of them for all they provided for Harper and for me postpartum. They also helped me burn a ton of calories from all the milk production to get the rest of my body into shape.

I hope you get the same appreciative feeling about yours, no matter their shape and size post-production, after learning about how amazing they are and all that they do to support you and your baby.

Another side effect of stopping your milk supply is that your period may come back. Due to the hormones produced during the breast-feeding process, you may not ovulate or have a period. Once you stop breastfeeding, your hormones will normalize, and your ovulation cycle will kick back in. Remember, it is still possible to get pregnant postpartum, even if you are lactating or your cycle has not returned.

It took about three months after I fully stopped producing for my period to come back. For some women, it is almost immediate and can even happen while they breastfeed. If you were still enjoying missed visits from "Aunt Flow", she will likely return soon after you stop producing breast milk.

No matter the style in which you feed your baby, take the time to realize how strong and capable you are throughout this process. Your main goal is to nurture your baby and if you are doing that, you are a good mom.

Along the way, don't beat yourself up over societal pressures. Pressures around the way your body looks, what it can or can't do, how long you use breast milk or formula, or if you go five days without showering because you are just trying to get by. You are doing the best you can with what you have, and your baby will love you for it. While they cannot say it to you with words, they will show it to you from the cuddles they give, their cries to be with you, and their milk-drink smiles and "coos" after they feel full and warm.

CHAPTER SIX

Partnership

The group of people that you rely on to help raise your child or support you can take many forms postpartum. That group can include a spouse, close family, distant family, friends that are like family, hired help, neighbors, community groups, and more. Some of you may be doing this on your own without a specific partner, but you will likely have a core set of people that will show up for you and your baby the most. If that is you, I hope you take some of the themes of the next section to help in your relationships with those core people in your life that help you along your mothering journey.

For some, like me, you have a specific partner to raise your child with. Your relationship with your partner can experience pressure during your postpartum time together. Both of you are experiencing something so new. You both can prepare as much as possible, but nothing you do beforehand will truly do justice to the experience of your new role as parents.

While you both will have to tackle this new life while sleep-deprived, many experiences will be different between the two of you. For example:

- Your partner has not experienced your baby like you did

during pregnancy. You built a bond while growing your tiny human that your partner will have to grow starting after birth. When your baby comes, this will be the first time that they can really physically interact with your baby (feeling in-womb kicks or hiccups doesn't really count). It is probably the first time that their parenting journey "feels real".

- Your partner will not be going through childbirth or the physical healing from that process afterward.

- Your partner will not experience the hormonal changes and feelings that you will. They will not be aware of them while they happen if you tell them.

- Your partner will not experience your complicated relationship with your body and how it will evolve over the coming months.

- Your partner will not experience the strain of breastfeeding, pumping, or drying up. While it may look easy, the mental load is taxing, you will constantly be hungry and need fluids, and experience discomfort.

- Your partner may need help understanding the mental load of planning or organizing everything on top of baby duties. From the doctor visits, the stress of keeping the schedule, and coordinating friends, family, and your baby, or even their innocent questions. It takes a toll when they ask where the baby socks are when you've shown him before, they have been in the same place for six months, he didn't look first, and the drawer they are in is clearly labeled.

- Your partner may not experience the need for physical space from another person's touch since your baby's need for your body can take a toll. Sometimes, you will just crave that physical space, especially if breastfeeding.

Since your partner's experience will be different than yours, clear communication is the only way they can truly understand your needs.

Remember, your partner is also tired. This is also new for them. They can also be overwhelmed, feel insecure in their parenting, and struggle to bond with their baby. They may not know how to help, or they may feel like a burden. Like you, they are also realizing how different their life will be moving forward. Communication must go both ways.

Communication

A few weeks before Harper arrived, Ryan and I discussed family member visitation. He asked about having his family come stay with us right after Harper was born and I was torn. We love his family and obviously wanted them to meet Harper right away. However, there were Covid protocols, so they were not allowed to visit the hospital. I knew that those first few days at home were going to be hard as well. I knew I would want privacy as we figured parenting out (and that I would likely be shirtless a lot for meals on demand!). I knew, no matter how much Ryan and his family said it didn't matter, that I would feel pressure to be a good host and provide for them during their stay. It felt overwhelming.

Ryan and I made time to talk through our feelings, logistical considerations, and communication plan to our family. We agreed that it would be too much to host them right after we came home, so we devised a few other options. Option one was to wait a month or so until we had a routine established for them to stay. Option two was to get them a hotel and let them visit in shorter time frames during the day when we were ready based on all our schedules. We also discussed how to talk through the plan with our family so they would understand the background. Having that conversation before Harper arrived was a huge relief and set us all up for a truly special family visit after Harper was born.

To set the groundwork for a strong partnership throughout your postpartum journey, start working on your communication now. Talk to your partner about the challenges of postpartum. Talk to them about your fears and ask them to be open and honest about theirs. Practice open listening where, instead of forming your response while they are still talking, just listen, digest everything they have said, and then respond. Monitor your reactions to each other to see if they are encouraging and supportive or if they are judgmental, managerial, or more about you versus your partner.

One of the struggles Ryan and I had in our communication was that he sometimes felt like I was his manager instead of his wife. I have a larger leadership role at work, and I tend to take charge and give direct guidance on how to do things, especially when I am tired. I recognize it as my "go-mode" and feel myself getting into that mode when I have a ton to do and feel stressed. I end up being very straightforward and provide directions of how and when to do something instead of just listening and being warmer in my communication.

Often, Ryan is looking for something other than direction when we communicate. When I responded with directions, I didn't portray confidence that he could take care of Harper on his own correctly.

While our approaches were different, his way of working was just fine too. Most often, Ryan wanted me to listen to what he had to say and be supportive instead of trying to solve everything for him.

It took several conversations for me to understand the difference in how I was communicating and what he actually needed. Then, I needed to identify when I was in "go-mode" and being managerial in our conversations and change my approach. Changing my habits didn't happen overnight, especially if we were rushed or tired. It took trial and error, but being receptive to Ryan's feedback and adjusting how we communicate has made our communication less transactional and more about active listening and encouragement.

When you are tired, stressed, and going through postpartum, communication can get even harder as you may not have the patience or energy to work as hard to communicate thoughtfully. Setting the foundation for expectations and good habits in your communication as far ahead of your baby's arrival will set you up for a better experience throughout your journey together. It is never too late to start that work and is always worth the effort. Being open to your partner's feedback in your communication and working on that together will make you both more successful as a team when times get tough.

I was also very open and honest in communicating with Ryan about how I felt as my emotions and body changed. Unless I told him, he would not have known I had mastitis. I let him feel the hard, red, lump on my breast where the clog was. The expression on his face was enough for me to know he sympathized with my plight.

I wasn't embarrassed when he felt the sheets on my side of the bed after I drenched them with sweat. He needed to feel my experiences to know their depth.

When I burst into tears, I told him that I didn't know what I was crying about but that I just needed to let my emotions go. My tears were not because I was happy or sad or because of anything he did. They were not about him or anything he could control. My tears were an outlet for the emotional release I needed.

Don't be embarrassed or shy with your partner about how you are doing postpartum. Honesty and openness will help them understand what you are going through, encourage empathy, and improve your communication.

There are also going to be times of communication breakdown or frustration. This is when the communication work you've done and your self-awareness is relied upon most.

When Harper was about four months old, Ryan was tired and stressed and started complaining about his job of bottle cleaning while standing over the sink, scrubbing bottles. He said bottle cleaning was just as hard as breastfeeding and implied breastfeeding was easier because I got to sit on the couch while doing so. Oh boy, did some resentment and rage start to build.

"How could he even fathom that those two things were the same?" I thought. Ryan knew how bad my three cases of mastitis were and all the issues we had with nipple shields and pumping. He knew that I woke up every morning from soreness due to swelling after just four hours of straight sleep. He saw me sprint into the kitchen to get my pumps, milk catcher and / or Harper to alleviate the milk build-up. At the time of this comment, I had a swollen, cracked nipple from the wrong flange size I was using, which was immensely painful, and I still had to express it. Plus, I had to maintain and stick to the schedule. I couldn't just avoid my job and let the milk stack up like bottles in the sink without painful repercussions!

While I could go on with all my very valid points as to why that statement was so frustrating, I also had to think about Ryan's point of view. While my feelings were valid, so were his. His experience was just different from mine. If I were in his shoes, I would also get tired of cleaning bottles and pump parts for over an hour a day, especially after working all day and being tired. His hands were dry from all that soap and scrubbing. While not done in the style I preferred, he was trying to relate to me. He couldn't fully understand how I felt. To his point, I was sitting on the couch watching a trashy Netflix show while he was doing the dishes looking out into the dark from the kitchen sink window. He was doing his job, which helped us both, and he had a right to express his stress just as much as I did.

Just like how I gave myself grace, I needed to extend that grace to Ryan. While I had so much to say about how it was "totally not the same", I just replied, "I get it". It took energy to pause, put myself in his shoes, and remove my ego. I actively chose to let it go and be the supportive partner he needed at that time. I did not want to demotivate him. He was doing his job and doing it excellently. That calls for encouragement, not the opposite. The rest of that night could have gone downhill but letting "it go" led to a nice, relaxed evening where we felt like a team.

While I have let it go, "a woman never forgets". As you might be able to tell, I still get a little heated when thinking about the conversation and my memory of the night comes to me vividly. But I use that night to guide how I react to our ongoing conversations. I understand my point of view, I put myself in Ryan's shoes, and I think about the outcomes of my options:

1. Reacting too quickly which will likely cause issues and re-sentment.
2. Thinking about both sides and, if it does require a conver-sation, addressing the situation with the goal of a positive, open conversation.
3. Being just a supportive listener by allowing my partner to vent their frustrations with no judgment or ego.
4. Acknowledging his point of view and letting it go.

Then I move forward.

Remember, while much of the postpartum hardship will be on your shoulders, your partner will also experience challenges. The main takeaway is to be thoughtful throughout your communication with your partner and try to put yourself in their shoes, just like they need to do for you.

Shared Responsibilities

Outside of communication with your partner or support system, the tactical items need to be discussed. While historically, moms have typically taken on the brunt of the parenting work, that should not be the standard and, thankfully, that is starting to change!

One of my close mom-friends introduced me to the concept of the "default parent," where all the parental work defaults to one par-ent specifically. Typically, because of longstanding societal norms, the default parent has been the mom. For some moms, there is just the in-stinct to handle everything for the child, especially in frustrating times. This further perpetuates the cycle where the other parent pulls back and is not proactive in their help moving forward.

You do not want to be the "default parent." To avoid that, don't do your partner's share of the parenting work. Use shared tracking apps for feeding, napping, and changing schedules so that both of you are aware of what needs to be done and when. Bring your partner in to help you put the baby's laundry away, so they get to know where everything goes and help organize in the future. Ask them to pick out your baby's outfit for the day and, even if it doesn't match, praise them, and let your baby wear "the look" so that your partner's confidence grows. In all likelihood, that outfit will be changed in a few hours after a blowout anyway.

The goal is to build your partner's confidence in planning and doing the baby tasks. Planning those tasks will alleviate your mental load, and doing will alleviate your physical load. Talk with your partner about the different roles you can have in your baby's care and set your parenting jobs. That way, you will have equal parenting vs default parenting.

In our pre-baby life, I made our food, and Ryan did all the cleanup afterward. Each of us would relax while the other worked. Once Harper came, that did not change. I did all the breastfeeding, pumping, milk storage, milk prep, and bottle making, while Ryan got some down time. Ryan cleaned and sanitized all the pump parts and the bottles. While I did want to help clean up in the kitchen, I knew I had to take my time to rest, job-free, and let him help how he could.

I've mentioned before how Ryan and I divided up the night shift to allow us each to get a block of sleep. In the early days, Ryan was sometimes tempted to stay awake and keep me company during my night shift. He just wanted to be helpful, but I knew that it was more critical to our collective success for him to get sleep during his sleep time. While it was so nice to have him by me while I did my tasks, we set our boundaries to make sure one of us got rest when the other couldn't.

Setting the boundaries during your on-call or rest times helps prevent guilt or resentment from building up. Sometimes the "Well, I helped you during my rest time" narrative can build up and cause a feeling of unfairness. If a partner does go above and beyond, set the expectation that the other party does not also have to go above and beyond if they don't have the energy or capacity to do so. The "tit-for-tat" expectation can disrupt a strong partnership.

Ryan and I also attended all Harper's doctor visits together. We would make a list of questions together beforehand to ensure we were on the same page and covered everything we needed. Ryan would order the vitamins or pick up prescriptions for Harper after each visit, and I would oversee scheduling the next one. Once Harper needed other appointments, we split the job of who was making appointments for which visit and the time-consuming job of finding and choosing the doctor's offices. Knowing Ryan was on top of his specific jobs, even if his scheduling methods or timelines were different from mine, was a great relief. While what worked for our partnership may not work for others, the idea is to communicate together to create a schedule that works for your collective family.

We talked about our system of delegating roles before Harper came, and that made all the difference. Of course, there were exceptions to the rules we established, and we did change up our duties as our circumstances changed, but having clear roles helped. Writing your roles down on a paper or whiteboard helps keep track of duties and accountability.

The Schedule

You and your partner also need to talk about your new family' schedule (consisting of baby's and parent's needs) and commit to being supportive of that schedule. From napping to feeding to changing to dishes to eating to showering to hopefully sleeping, there is a lot to keep track of. A consistent routine is proven to help your baby nap better and sleep longer. It will also help with your mental load. Ensuring that you and your partner stick to the schedule and discussing and aligning on any deviations to that schedule together will help you keep organized and lower the stress.

Outside of your baby's needs, there are two other critical components to add to your schedule:

1. Time together for you and your partner to bond
2. Time apart for you and your partner focus on your individual needs

Overall, making a schedule, having guidelines, and openly talking about responsibilities, goals, your relationship, and your individualism will help you build a stronger foundation for a much more positive experience.

Bonding Time

It is easy to get caught up with "all things baby" and let your relationship with your partner get lost along the way. While it may not seem like it, given all the chaos, postpartum is an ideal time to grow your bond with your partner. Look at all the ways you work as a solid team throughout the challenges you face together!

Did you both just survive a "poo-pocalypse"? Did you both just sneak out of the baby's room successfully without waking them from their nap? Did you both finish your chores and flop on the couch after a long day? Did you both just "survive" the day? Did one of you forget to pack an extra outfit, causing the other to take off and use their men's size large undershirt as a dress for your 5-month-old daughter in a Thai restaurant after a massive blowout?

Prevailing over all those challenges deserves attention as you overcome them together. Those challenges build strength in a partnership and provide memories to laugh about for years to come. Those are the times that illustrate why you decided to embark on this journey together in the first place.

Ryan and I established a routine for the evening. Once I was physically able to, we went on evening walks with Harper in the stroller and our dog, Beans. We would talk about our days, our upcoming plans, or just take some quiet time to enjoy some fresh air together. We would return home and make dinner between pumping/feeding/napping schedules. Harper would usually go down for bed and then we would eat dinner together. We started asking each other two questions each night at dinner:

1. How are you doing emotionally?
2. What are you grateful for today?

These two questions encouraged openness and allowed us to check in with each other's mental state. They also made us reflect on the day and usually resulted in us being grateful for the other person's support or the health and happiness of Harper. We would discuss cute things Harper did or milestones she had and reiterate that we were baffled we made someone so wonderful. It made us value the time we had and genuinely recognize one another's growth as a parent and as a partner.

After dinner, we would relax on the couch together. While our own thoughts or the TV may have occupied us, we were still connected until the 8:30-9 PM feeding, and pumping routine kicked off.

Some of our parent friends make more formal plans to bond. They have a babysitter scheduled for the third Saturday of each month, rain or shine. This allows them to build their connection on a set schedule with accountability and improves their intimacy and general partnership.

While Ryan and I didn't formalize anything like that (yet—this could change!), the important message here is to find ways to set aside time that prioritizes building your bond. A healthy bond will help both of you show up stronger as partners and parents.

Me Time

Individual time is essential for your wellbeing. I've heard stories or watched shows where people "lose themselves" through their parenting journey because they dedicate 100% of their time to others. It is surprisingly easy to do if you don't make a concerted effort to nurture yourself. This is especially important for single parents who bare so much more of the workload burden. While the task of finding time and scheduling the help required to support you during your time may be daunting, there are ways to make it work.

That time can look different for everyone. Whether it is an hour a week for a hobby, time every day for a long shower, or an extra nap here and there. You and your support system need to make, agree on, and be supportive of time for you to focus on your individualization.

Ryan plays softball with his co-workers on Wednesdays. He loves it. We made it a priority for him to play, even after Harper came. If the weather and my health permitted, Harper and I cheered him on at his games. The smile on his face when his little girl arrived at that first game was priceless. He was so excited to introduce her to his coworker. Those games also got me out of the house and into some fresh air. Harper seemed fascinated by her new surroundings. Ryan's individual time was beneficial for all of us.

I also needed time to exercise and relieve stress. On Saturday mornings, Ryan would watch Harper for as long as I needed to get my workout in. It helped me build my body confidence and distress from the week. He also watched her, without question, when I went to dinner with the girls. He even pushed me to go on short, overnight work trips to help advance my career.

We know that supporting each other's goals outside of our daughter and our relationship helps build our bond and make our lives more fulfilling. It also allows us to showcase what a strong, supportive partnership looks like to our daughter.

Your individual needs and support may look very different than mine. That is OK. The goal is to make sure you identify what you need, how often you need it, how long it takes, and how you can get the help you need to get that time for yourself.

Sex-pectations

While sex after pregnancy can be an emotional and sensitive topic to discuss with your partner, it needs to be discussed.

Physically, your doctor will typically give you the go-ahead to start having sex at your six-week postpartum appointment. There are many reasons for the six-week wait, and it is vital to set the right expectations for timelines with your partner.

The first reason is that the most important healing process postpartum takes place two to three weeks after birth. Your uterine lining and any vaginal tearing are healing, and your cervix is closing. Sex during this time would drastically hinder that healing process and can cause postpartum hemorrhaging or uterine infection.

Additionally, if you had a C-section, you should not engage your abdominal wall. It takes time and patience to heal. You do not want to disrupt or infect your incision.

You can also get pregnant as quickly as three weeks after you give birth. As mentioned, doctors typically recommend waiting a year before your subsequent pregnancy so your body can heal and be prepared for the next one.

Because of the changes in your hormones, especially if you are breastfeeding, you will likely have dryness, causing the tissues of the vagina to be dry and thin. Without the right lubrication, the dryness can lead to very difficult and painful experiences for potentially the longevity of your breastfeeding journey.

Outside of the physical challenges, you may not be emotionally ready. You may be exhausted, have lost confidence, or feel scared after all your body just went through. You may have a multitude of other emotions tied to your body and sex. All those emotions, thoughts, and feelings are natural to experience.

Remember, your partner will only know how you are feeling, physically or mentally, with clear communication.

To set you and your partner up for a successful and enjoyable experience for both parties, discuss this topic even before you give birth. Talk about how you will need to wait six weeks and that, even after six weeks, you may need to assess your feelings and if it is the right time. If you are not ready to go all the way, discuss other ways to be intimate with one another that both of you will be excited about and comfortable with.

When you are ready to go all the way, set the expectation that you will need to control the pace and that there is a chance you may need to stop if it is not working. Prepare and use the right products to make it as comfortable as possible. Communicate your needs clearly during the process.

Remember, you are in a partnership. You chose this person to go on this journey together. You will need to lean on each other for support, through thick and thin, through poop and spit up, through the adorable moments that make you cry happy tears and scary moments in which you both need each other's strength. Don't get so caught up in parenting that you forget why you chose each other. Make time to work on your communication. Through that communication, frequently share your respect, love, and appreciation of one another. Despite the hardships, you will be on this parenting journey together for the rest of your lives. Cherish it and each other together.

CHAPTER SEVEN
Work & Care

At some point in your postpartum journey, you must decide what your career future looks like. You have recently been promoted to the most exciting job in the world, motherhood, but you will also need to decide if your new job title is a "stay-at-home mom", "working mom", or something in between.

Stay-At-Home Mom

Historical portrayals and stereotypes of SAH moms perpetuate a very unrealistic narrative. A narrative where you joyfully sing around the house while cleaning all day, care for and teach perfectly behaved kids, cook perfectly plated multi-course meals for breakfast, lunch, and dinner with ingredients pulled from the garden you tend, and one in which you are always in a pleasant, energy filled mood when the breadwinner comes home. They relax after dinner while you clean up and put the kids to bed, and your life is Instagram perfect.

The reality is very, very different. Staying at home and being the caregiver for your child is messy, stressful, can be lonely, and not easy. In fact, in 2018, Welch's conducted a study of two thousand moms that found that being a mom is the equivalent of not one, but two and a half full-time jobs (CBS 19 News, 2021).

Most mom shifts start at 6:23 AM and go until 8:31 PM, meaning a fourteen-hour workday with only one hour of reported "alone time." Not only that, but SAH moms don't get weekends off. Four out of ten of those moms surveyed reported that they felt their days were a "never-ending series of tasks." Also, the study did not include overnight time for moms who still had little ones up in the middle of the night, meaning those fourteen hours are under-reporting.

If that study tells you anything, it is that being a stay-at-home mom is a very intensive, extremely important job. If anyone makes you feel differently, they are in the wrong, not you. You are bringing up your child while also running and maintaining your household. You should be proud of the life you are building and confident that dedicating so much of your time to that endeavor is a fantastic feat.

While there will be many stressors, you will make so many memories with your little one and impart so much love while you are with them. You will get to watch them hit all their milestones. You will get to shape their worldview. You will get to help them learn about the world and its wonders. You will get to teach them to walk, talk, read, and be curious. You will help them grow into who they will become.

While you are dedicating so much time to your baby, as mentioned, it is imperative to maintain your "time for you". You must find time in your day to remember who you are outside of your child. Build time into your week for activities that stimulate you. Don't just skip your "me time" because something else came up. Maintaining "you" will make you a better mom, reduce resentment for your partner who gets to get away and have an outside life, improve your confidence, and ensure that you do not lose yourself.

You will also need socialization with adults, not just kids. There can be a lot of loneliness in raising a child at home by yourself. Make sure you build in time with your friends, family, social groups, and anyone who can stimulate you mentally with good conversation and activities you enjoy. Doing so will help you keep your sanity.

Other parent friends are a great option, especially if they have kids around your child's age, have a home that is also child-proof, can have play dates throughout the day, and live close by. If you need to build your mom-friend network, you can meet them at the park, through on-line mom social groups in your area, on walks in your neighborhood, at the library, or even the local recreation center. Get out of the house and find a community to support both you and your kiddo.

I went a little stir-crazy while I was on maternity leave. Every day felt like Groundhog Day in our house. We had the same schedule, I didn't do my hair or makeup, I wore "I don't really care" clothes daily, and we stayed inside the house for what felt like 23 of the 24 hours. I was not myself, and I was not that happy.

Something needed to change, so made of list of how to improve my days. The list started with taking an extra ten minutes to get ready in the mornings by myself instead of rushing out of the bedroom to see Ryan and Harper. I told Ryan that Friday and Saturday nights were our "nights out" to eat so we could get out of the house. I walked outside twice a day in different locations, one just in the neighborhood and one that I needed to drive to for a change of scenery. I started taking Harper to my parent's house at least once during the week. We would either hang out with my parents, or my mom would watch Harper while I went shopping, got my nails done, or napped. I got together with at least one group of friends, with or without Ryan and

Harper, on the weekend. I always had my hour to work out on Saturday mornings.

All these things diversified my weeks, changed my surroundings, pushed me to be social, and improved my mood so I could be a better mom to Harper and partner to Ryan.

Many SAH parents feel like they have lost their identity in their new role. They don't make the time they need to nurture their individual selves. Whether it is joining a local parent group, starting yoga around the house, learning to play tennis, volunteering, taking up knitting or quilting, playing a video game, or writing a book, having a hobby or activity just for you can help you find your identity. Those things give you a goal, you can see improvement as you continue investing time into them, and they provide joy. If you find yourself in a rut, identify those things that you need to be happy, that give you a sense of self, and make sure to make time to do them. You are worthy and deserving of that time and attention.

Another surprising SAH aspect that may feel overwhelming is your new role as a teacher. You need to learn all the ways to help your child develop. There are so many milestones as your baby gets older. From learning to roll over, doing tummy time so your baby builds neck strength, learning when to transition to food outside of breast milk or formula, to teaching sign language so that your baby can communicate before they become verbal, there is a long list of things to teach and stages to reach. You will need to learn how to help your child achieve those milestones and what tools to use while weeding through all the conflicting advice on the best way to do X, Y, Z.

The education process is also ongoing. Once your child hits one milestone, it is time to work on the next. You only have limited time to research and learn yourself. It can be a lot of pressure. Tapping into your parent network, asking your pediatrician for learning resources, filtering through social media, and finding educational books and tools can all help on both your child's and your educational path.

Going Back to Work

Maternity leave in the US is far too short without enough support. Some women only get four to eight weeks of maternity leave, which is barely enough time to heal. Many women may not be paid during that time or only paid portions of their typical income. Many of the jobs we go back to are in-person, on your toes, or physical in nature.

Before having a baby, I didn't realize that maternity leave wasn't just for healing and bonding with your baby. So much of it has to do with nourishing your baby and feeding them breast milk. Many jobs do not have an area for privacy or for sanitary pumping. Many jobs do not allow sufficient breaks within the work shift to take the time needed to pump. Many jobs provide the right policies but put on social pressure that does not provide the right support. As a result, many new moms end their pumping or breastfeeding journeys when they return to work.

Switching to formulas should not be a choice we have to make so quickly in our child's life for something that makes such a large impact on their development. Not only that, but formula is expensive when breast milk is free (outside of the time and body commitment already discussed.)

Maternity leave in America should be guaranteed, longer, and more supportive of women and their babies. There. I said it. It needed to be said and recognized. Now we can move on.

It can be daunting or exciting if you decide to return to work. It does mean you get to interact with more people that are your age, get back into some of the pre-baby routine, reestablish your financial situation, and work on your career aspirations. It also means the end of your 24/7 bonding with your little one. Whether your partner is taking leave, you're doing in-home care, hiring a nanny, using your grandparents or family, enrolling in daycare, or other, it will be a transition period, and you will need to establish a new routine.

In addition to the schedule aspects, don't be surprised if your relationship with work changes. Pre-baby, you may have focused on your career growth and invested the time and mental capacity to drive that growth. Once you have a baby, your priorities may change to support maximizing your time with your baby.

Ryan and I quickly realized that, based on our work schedules, we would only get about an hour in the morning and one and a half to two hours with Harper at night. Those two and a half to three hours we had with her were also filled with tasks, so the quality time with Harper was much less than that.

We made a conscious effort to be present with Harper during our limited time and make the most of it. That meant that the one to two extra hours I used to put towards my workday were now Harper's hours. Once I logged off to pick Harper up from daycare, phone time, especially checking messages and emails, was limited until she went to bed.

My priority is Harper, and my work style, while still important, needed to adapt to my priority. While I may have checked an email or two, I did not add on those extra hours of work after Harper went to bed, either. I needed enough sleep to be the best mom I could be and have my brain fully function during work hours. I also needed time to relax. I can be a fantastic mom and grow in my career, but the pace at which I grow would likely slow down to accommodate the reallocation of my time.

In my career, I've seen and heard about far too many women who come back from maternity leave earlier than planned, sacrifice time with their babies and end breastfeeding earlier than planned because of work guilt or pressure. While their companies may have thanked them verbally for doing so, they weren't promoted any sooner or incentivized financially to do so. They would have received the same treatment if they had taken the time they needed and worked just what was required. I'm not saying you shouldn't go above and beyond or that all companies are like that. What is essential is to make sure your added time at work is worth the cost of time with your family.

Don't be embarrassed about being a mom at work, either. Your work may not provide the necessary physical or timing spaces, so you must make them and be unapologetic about them.

If there is no room for pumping in privacy, make one by taking over a room and putting paper in the window. If there is no sink to wash pump parts, do it in the community kitchen. If no kitchen is available, talk to HR or management about what you need and how they can accommodate your needs.

Don't be afraid to speak up. We need to normalize motherhood and all its challenges. Society expects us to be perfect moms but doesn't give us the required tools to succeed. We need to make those spaces and make them visible. It may be uncomfortable, but your effort will help normalize and get support for all the moms to come.

In the US, the Fair Labor Standards Act (FLSA) protects most nursing employees by protecting the right to reasonable break time and a place, other than a bathroom, that is shielded from view to express breast milk while at work. This right is available for up to one year after the child's birth. If your employer is not providing the needed time and space, therefore violating your rights, you can file a complaint and seek damages through the Wage and Hour Division of the Department of Labor (U.S. Department of Labor Wage and Hour Division, 2022).

I went on a work trip six months into mom life. I pumped on the plane, sitting next to some very nice gentlemen. There was no pumping room in the office, so I found an empty room and turned away from the glass door white I pumped. I shamelessly cleaned all my supplies in the open-concept kitchen sink and left them on the drying rack for anyone who walked into the office to see. All my milk either went into the communal freeze, fridge, or into a cooler with ice packs that I brought with me. I had to move all the mini-bar items out of my hotel room fridge to store my milk at night and talked to the front desk to make sure they didn't charge me for the items I moved around.

I also went to a vendor's office on that trip. I asked the vendor, in advance, to book a pumping room on their campus. Mid-meeting, one of our vendors walked me down to the nursing room. She had to get another new mom who worked at the company to badge me into the room because they didn't typically allow non-employees to access the nursing rooms. That strategy worked for my first pump of the day, but I did not have access to that room for the second. Again, I had to go into a spare room. This time it had a massive fishbowl window in it. Thankfully, the room had big, red swivel chairs, so I pumped in a very visible space facing the wall while checking emails. I carried a cooler with long-lasting ice packs with me throughout the day in a large backpack to store the milk I pumped.

All this was very inconvenient and a bit stressful to figure out. But, along the way, many employees who saw what I was doing commended what I was doing. Strangers asked me about my baby and how motherhood was going. I talked openly about the experience of traveling as a new mom and the challenges. All my co-workers and vendors were supportive of me as well. When I stepped out of meetings to go pump, they didn't ask questions. My team just caught me up when I returned.

You can be a mom, career-driven, and advance at work. You will just need to reassess how you accomplish your goals and the pace at which you accomplish those goals based on how you reprioritize your time.

Work Expectations

If you are continuing to breastfeed and pump while working, you will need to set your boundaries and expectations with your human resources team, boss, co-workers, and clients. Start to formulate your plan and talk to your support system a few days before going to work so that you can set expectations with a plan that fits within your work schedule immediately. A few items you will want to consider:

- What is your childcare schedule? Do you have pick-up and drop-off duties? Does your childcare span the entire day? Will you need to tweak your work schedule to accommodate care, or will your partner, friends, or family help?

- How does your care schedule impact your commute or

previous work routines?

- Are you still pumping? If so, when are the set times you will want to do that every day, how many times, and how long? Where will this occur? Will you need to ask your employer for accommodations? How will you store the milk that you have pumped? Do you have backup breast pads to soak up leakage?

- What is your backup plan if you do not have care on a workday? If your caregiver needs a sick day or if daycare is closed for a holiday where your work is not, what is your backup plan? If your child is sick and needs to stay home on a workday, what is your backup plan?

- If you previously traveled for work, do you still want to travel as much moving forward? If not, how many days and how long are you willing to go for? When would that first trip ideally be?

Depending on your employer, there may be policies around work flexibility, pumping, childcare assistance, and other parent-based support. It is worth exploring those options and knowing the policies when you return.

My 8 AM wake-up routine went bye-bye when I went back to work. My workday went from eight to five, and Ryan's was nine to six. Because of our new time frames, we had to update our approach to sleep and when our day started.

With both of our work schedules in mind, we decided to start our day at six. We would change Harper, give her a bottle, and go for a dog walk. Ryan would leave to drop Harper off at seven, and I would have time for chores or a workout before starting my day at eight.

On my first day back to work, I set 30-minute daily blocks on my work calendar at 9:30 AM, 12:30 PM, and 3:30 PM for pumping. I made sure that no one scheduled meetings during that time. I also had a calendar block at 5:15 PM so I could leave to pick Harper up at daycare by 5:30. We would come back, bathe Harper, and go for a family walk. I cooked dinner, Harper went to bed at 6:30-7, Ryan cleaned dishes and bottles, we had our hour of relaxation together, I pumped and made bottles for the next day's daycare, Harper came back out for her 8:30-9 PM bottle, and then it was bedtime for all us.

We started this routine about a week before I returned to work, and I immediately implemented my work schedule expectations when I went back to work. Everyone (Harper, Ryan, and my work) knew what to expect from me, and it gave me the flexibility I needed to stay sane, get everything done, and plan our days.

Mentally, there can be the general work-induced stress, anxiety of managing both a home and work and some added guilt for not being a SAH mom. Some of the challenges we did not anticipate were around care coverage when daycare was closed or when Harper was sick.

One of the cons of daycare is that germs are rampant. They spread so easily from kid to kid and then, inevitably, to you. There is a cycle of sickness from daycare to your child, to mom, and then to the next person in the virus conga line. Once everyone in the line gets it and starts to recover, the next round of infection hits. You may have been a relatively healthy person before becoming a parent, but those days of clear noses, constant energy, and 100% brain function are likely going to be gone for a few years.

When Harper got sick, she would have to stay home from daycare until she was better. Because our baby is very generous, she generously shared her colds with us. Having a sick child, especially one that is only a few months old, can be scary, heart-wrenching, and sleep-depriving. Managing a sick kiddo while being under the weather and trying to figure out how to work or take off work at the same time can be overwhelming. The good thing is, it will pass, and all your coworkers, especially those with kids, will understand. These things happen. Make a tentative sick-day plan for coverage with your partner, alternate caretakers, and work, so you are prepared.

At first, the guilt of sending Harper to daycare was hard to deal with. Before I returned to work, I knew it would be hard but that it would be worth it. By working, I demonstrated to Harper that moms could be successful, strong leaders with careers they can be proud of, and help support their families financially. While I would have less total time with Harper, I would ensure that my time with Harper was quality time.

I want Harper to know that, while difficult, there is a balance you can strike to raise a supportive family and be there for your family while also achieving your personal goals. I want Harper to have a strong work ethic while also having a work-life balance because, for us, work is not the most important thing in life. By choosing to chase your dreams in a way that also prioritizes your family, you can show your child that they can too.

My reasons for returning to work helped with the guilt I felt, but daily life and interactions still triggered it occasionally. When the daycare teachers kept reminding me that Harper was the first baby in her class to be dropped off in the morning, I felt guilty that other moms got more time with their kids, and I felt sad thinking that Harper might notice that she was in daycare longer than her peers. When daycare had parties at three in the afternoon for Valentine's Day, Easter, Thanksgiving Day, and other holidays throughout the year which were hard to accommodate because of work, I felt guilty at the thought of not attending and so stressed about fitting those parties into my schedule. When we had a rushed morning, and Harper's 6-9M size pants were in the wash, so she wore the clean 3-6M size pants that fit more like capris and definitely did not match the rest of her outfit, I felt guilty seeing some of the other kids dressed perfectly.

But here is the thing. Harper didn't notice or understand that she was the first at daycare because she was four months old. For those parties, I showed up when I could, and the massive smile, clapping, and happy scream that she greeted me with was enough to melt my stress away. Harper had no idea her pants were capris, and they were quickly changed when she got to daycare because she had a blowout. Those other kids with perfect outfit days had capri days too!

I know for a fact that I am not a perfect mom, but I am a good mom. I try my best and, for the things that matter the most, I show up, I am present, and I give Harper the support she needs. That is enough.

In the grand scheme of things, all that guilt was self-inflicted and didn't matter. Don't let it eat you up. Be there for your baby when it matters and give yourself grace for those other stresses that don't matter. When you find yourself in similar situations or feel the mom guilt creeping up, remind yourself that what you are doing is enough.

Overall, going back to work can be stressful and come with social pressure. Set yourself up for success by creating a plan, talking to your partner about roles and support, communicating expectations for work from your first day back, and giving yourself grace.

Child Care

Harper started daycare when she was four months old. Ryan and I dressed her up and dropped her off together. We both cried when we gave her to her teacher and walked away. We both worked from home, and when we came out of our offices, we both talked about how we missed her and checked the daycare app frequently to see updates and photos. We did appreciate the time to ourselves, though.

The change hit home when we picked Harper up from daycare that first day and she smelled different. Newborn babies have this wonderful smell. You just want to breathe them in all the time. After daycare, Harper smelled like a mix of daycare and her teacher. The difference from her usual smell made both of us sad. We realized that her life would now be significantly impacted by the outside world and that we would no longer be her whole world. We immediately bathed Harper and her smell went back to normal. While her smell was back, the experience changed us.

We did a daycare test run with Harper the Friday before I returned to work. This allowed us to test out what it would be like and handle the emotional difficulties before layering on the stress of a workday as well. Since we were not in a rush at drop off, we met her teachers and asked questions, making us more comfortable with the staff watching. At pick up, we talked to her teachers about how she did throughout the day and asked our remaining questions, giving us confidence for the days to come. The test run day also had a side benefit of allowing us to have solo time to knock out end-of-maternity leave tasks and mentally prepare for the next week.

If possible, do a test run with your care provider to ease the process of returning to work and ensure you are entirely comfortable with what to expect.

While the first few days were tough, we quickly realized how amazing daycare was for Harper. Her teachers loved her and taught her so much. She was using both hands to hold her own bottle by six months, walking at ten months, and signing her first "all-done" and "I'm hungry" signs right around her first birthday. All her quick progress was from seeing other kids in the classroom and from her vigilant teachers. While it was difficult to send her off every day and endure all the colds she picked up and shared with us along the way, we know that daycare was the right fit for her development and our work schedule.

Whatever childcare option you choose may be hard initially, but it will get easier over time.

CHAPTER EIGHT
Mindset

A few months into motherhood, I was introduced to the notion that the first interaction of the day sets the tone for the entire day. This is true for the first thoughts you think each day and the first communication, verbal or nonverbal, you have with your partner and child.

Waking up each morning and thinking to yourself, "today is going to be a good day," or rolling over towards or walking into the room with your partner and greeting them with a "Good morning, how are you?" can make a massive difference in your mindset and your starting interactions with your partner. It immediately puts you in a "can-do" mood, puts your partner into a neutral or positive disposition towards you, and helps you start the day on the right foot together.

Starting the day on a positive note is a small step and one that can be forgotten easily. When you are sleep deprived, wake up to a baby crying after only a few hours of sleep, still stewing over some chore you wish your partner would have done the night before, or are struggling with the baby blues, intentionally putting positive energy into your day right from the start (even if it is forced) can help you overcome so much.

Your mindset throughout postpartum, especially in the first few weeks, will be a big part of your overall experience. There are so many doubts, frustrations, emotions, social pressures, hormones, and relational issues that can arise, and your mindset for overcoming stressors will make an impact on how tough or how easy they are to get through. Postpartum is hard, and there is no doubt about it. But you have got this. You will get through it. You are a good mom.

I have always wanted two daughters. My sister and I have an incredible bond, and I want two daughters so that they can also become each other's best friend. We had Harper when I was 32, so I didn't want to wait more than a year before trying for another. Before Harper came, I had our timing all planned out and had talked at length to Ryan about it. He was hesitant to have Harper in the first place and was much more hesitant about my plan for number two up until delivery night.

When Harper came into this world, both of our perspectives changed. Only a few hours after Harper was delivered, Ryan looked at me, totally smitten, and said we needed to try again ASAP. "It is January. The doctors say we need to wait a year, so that means we can try in December. But it took us two years to get pregnant, so maybe we will start trying in October just in case it takes more time…" Ryan was all in for a second and couldn't contain his excitement.

My mind was in a completely different place than Ryan's. I looked down at my perfect baby, also smitten, but I completely lost all confidence in my strength to go through this again. In the first three weeks, I was up during those late-night feeds asking questions like: How will I get through postpartum? When will I get sleep? How can I handle all this stress? What if we only have one?

Postpartum was that hard. I had to use different techniques, like starting the day with a positive mindset, to get myself back into a positive headspace. I had to tell myself that "today is going to be a good day" each morning. I told myself, over and over, that each week would pass. With each week, postpartum would get easier, and it did get easier.

My emotions started to normalize, and my headspace went from foggy to clear within a few short weeks. There was a light at the end of the exhaustion tunnel. With the help of my partner, my friends, my family, the schedule, the internet, my overwhelming love for Harper, and my positive mindset, we made it through the tough days. Within one month, I was also doing the month-math for when we could and should start "trying" again.

Empathy

Another way to help with your overall mindset and mentality is through empathy. Empathy is when you try to understand someone else's experiences by imagining yourself in their situation. Since your baby cannot easily communicate with you, it is easy to get frustrated when trying to understand their needs. Having empathy can dissolve some of that frustration and help you ideate how to help.

When your baby is crying, it is likely because of a mix of the below simple reasons:

1. They are hungry.
2. They are tired.
3. They have a diaper that needs changing.
4. They need you for comfort and love.

The most common reasons babies cry aren't complicated. If you put yourself in your baby's shoes, you'd probably be crying and frustrated as well. Your baby needs something which they can't provide for themselves, and they are solely reliant on you to help them with it, but they can't communicate with you properly on what they need. They don't know why their tummy hurts from hunger, why their bum feels damp, or why they feel so tired. The only way they know how to improve their situation is to get your attention. That would be hard for anybody.

When you are tired and frustrated that your baby woke you up in the middle of the night crying or does not want to be put down, try to empathize with what they're going through on the other side. Most likely, they just need your love, comfort, and support to provide what they need as they learn this new world.

Harper cried for mainly one of two reasons; she was hungry or tired. When she cried, we would check the time and our apps to see where we were on our schedule for feedings or naps. If the most immediate solution didn't do the trick, we would just go through the checklist of the other things that she usually cried about and try to remedy each one while trying to soothe her at the same time.

Sometimes, Harper would get tummy issues from feeding, feel lousy, startle awake, or cry and nothing we did to help worked. In those cases, we just had to power through it with support. Those times were hard, but consciously empathizing with Harper helped with our overall mood and sometimes even gave us new ideas that calmed Harper down.

During those hard times, know that your baby just needs you or your help and is doing their best to communicate that to you.

Support System

Your support system of people who are there for you and your child postpartum play a massive part in keeping a positive mental state. From being your outlet for frustration, source of needed advice, helpful doers of tasks (like laundry, childcare, or providing a meal), to just being your excuse get out of the house, the people in your life will rally around you and try their best to alleviate some of the heavy load of parenthood.

Don't be shy about using the help that they offer. The old adage "it takes a village to raise a child" is well known for a reason. Don't try and do everything yourself. Those in your life who are already moms will know what you are going through best. Ask them for the help you need. In the end, getting the help you need will be better for both you and your baby and will likely make your support system happy that they could help as well.

Sometimes, your support network can be a little too helpful or too present. As a new mom, you will want time with just your new little family. You will want time to develop those bonds and new routines without outside pressure. While it may sound like a great idea to have family stay immediately postpartum to help, you may want to consider if you want privacy initially. Think about how much additional pressure visitors, especially ones that stay over, add to your mental load. If their presence isn't a big deal and usually relieves stress, have them stay. If there is even just the slightest bit of pressure, it may be best to establish boundaries upfront so that you get the time you need with your little family. It is perfectly acceptable to let your support system know they are welcome during the times or in the circumstances that work best for you and your baby.

As I mentioned earlier, we originally intended to have family stay with us right after coming home from the hospital. We love our family and wanted them to meet Harper as soon as they could. After talking through the details though, we realized that it would be far too stressful to have them stay with us so soon after birth. While we stressed over having the hard conversation our family, they understood and responded with love and empathy. When they did eventually visit, it was a much more enjoyable, stress-free reunion for all of us.

Your support system may also have different parenting or interaction approaches with your baby then you may prefer. If you have a structure for your child that you want your family or friends to follow, be clear about that from the start. That structure could be around nap times, feeding, how to play, safe sleep, tummy time, or any other preferences that you have about the care of your child.

Your baby's grandparents had different standards of safety when they raised their children, so make sure to give them updated information on how to care properly for your little one. While they may say, "I know this stuff. I raised you!" tell them lovingly that you want to raise your child as successfully as they raised you, and following your parenting style is how you will ensure that happens.

Neighbors and strangers may try to join your support system. They may walk up and want to talk to you and "ooh" and "ahh" over your little bundle of joy. Do not be shy about setting your physical boundaries with them. For some reason, strangers think they have the right to touch your child. They do not have that right. If someone approaches you and you do not want them to touch your baby's toes, little hands, head, or any other part, pull your baby away and ask them to look and not touch.

Harper came into this world during the COVID pandemic. Multiple people, strangers and acquaintances, came up to us during the pandemic without masks. Masked or not, people would get too close and would even reach out to touch Harper. I didn't want those people touching me, so why would I allow them to touch Harper? My hand would go out at lightning speed to block them, and I would say "you can look, but please don't touch." My response usually got a bit of a shocked reaction, but I didn't care. They do not have a right to touch my child. I would follow my directive with context that we were being cautious of Harper's health and then turn their attention to how cute Harper was. Harper would almost immediately elicit a smile from the other party, break the tension, and open conversation or allow for us to part ways.

In the US, the first round of most vaccines don't get administered until babies are two months old. If your baby gets a fever over 100.4 degrees and is under three months old, your doctor will advise that they go to the emergency room. A stranger or acquaintance with unwashed hands who may have a cold or other illness may get their feelings hurt from clear boundaries, but that is inconsequential considering the potentially severe consequences on your baby's health.

If you do not have people in your life that you can go to for advice and support, the internet can be of massive help. I am not talking about "Doctor Google" who may bring you down a rabbit hole of how a minor cold has the same symptoms of a life-threatening, incurable disease. I am talking about social media support groups.

During my pregnancy, I was using a Peloton bike to work out. While I was not involved in many groups before pregnancy, I found a "Peloton Preggos + Postpartum" group on Facebook early in my pregnancy which helped me through so many issues, questions, and anxieties.

In the first few months, I was just a reader in the group, learning about reviews of different products and tips about development during and after pregnancy. About halfway through my pregnancy, I was diagnosed with Placenta Previa, a condition where the placenta covers, partially covers, or is very close to the cervix (Mayo Clinic, Postpartum care, 2022). In some cases, Placenta previa can cause bleeding or preterm birth. When combined with my blood clotting disorder, it could potentially be life threatening.

The diagnosis scared me, and I found support through the Facebook group from other women with the same condition. While some of the more severe examples in the group caused me more concern, the group made me aware of all potential outcomes. Having other women around that could advise was immensely helpful and relieving.

I continue to use social groups for community, especially when I am in a bind. While I don't know the women in those groups personally, I can talk to, commiserate with, and learn from them. It is handy to have access to women in similar circumstances and with babies in the same development stages. While you may not be a big "social group" person, finding a village of support online can help you get through the rough times.

Note that advice is not always going to be helpful or wanted. There will be plenty of people proactively giving you their thoughts on how to parent in person or online. When advice came my way, I found it best just to nod, smile, say "thank you" and then take or leave advice based on how it fit into our parenting and lifestyle.

One common theme I have heard over and over in the unwanted

advice category is, "Enjoy this stage now because the next will have…
sleep regression, walking, the terrible twos, eating issues, until you have
another, the terror of threes" insert z,y,x stage and attach a negative
component to it.

For some reason, many people want to suggest that the next stage
is harder or worse than your current stage. That is absolutely incorrect. While it is true that every stage has its difficulties, every stage also
has massive rewards. For example:

- **Sleep regression:** As babies reach different developmental stages, their sleep patterns can change. This could
  wake them up in the middle of the night or require some
  shifts at bedtime. You have already handled so many sleep
  changes since birth and you can handle the changes to
  come. It will be OK and long nights of sleep will happen
  again. Also, some babies don't regress, or the regression
  does not last that long. There is no reason to dread something that may not ever happen.

- **Terrible twos:** Yes, you will experience tantrums, but
  also, your child says the cutest things, can walk around
  and help you, is developing speech, and is hitting so many
  other wondrous milestones. The trade-off of occasional
  fits while you get to experience your child's growth and
  all the other funny, quirky, and loveable things they do, is
  worth it.

- **Walking:** Yes, walking requires a whole new level of
  home-childproofing and watching; however, it is so fun to
  see your kiddo explore the world. There is almost nothing
  better than when your child sees you, smiles, and then runs

into your arms. While I have to follow Harper around the house almost all weekend and be her bumper guard for falls and she has fallen on her face and gotten booboos, the perks of playing hide and seek and seeing her become independent outweigh those things. I can't even begin to express how heart melting and fun it was when she started dancing to music as well!

Don't let other people's negative experiences of various stages build dred or cloud your future. While each stage has pros and cons, once a stage passes, you will likely miss it fondly. Try to cherish each part of the journey with those around you who lift you and your little up and support you along the way.

The Little Things

Parenting is a journey. It is about enjoying all the years you have with your child. While there will be major milestones, the little daily moments along the way make those core memories that last forever.

Instead of finding the inevitable inconveniences of parenting annoying or frustrating, try to laugh at the little things. You will get spit up on, peed on, pooped on, and snotted on. Food will get thrown across the kitchen, stuck in your hair, and get all over your baby's face. Milk will get spilt, will leak through your shirt, and will overflow in your bottle warmer, and smell gross. All these things will happen. It is how you react to them that matters and those little make lifelong, cherished memories.

Trying to keep a baby from getting messy is tough, so why not just let the mess happen? When Harper started eating solids, we took her to our favorite local Tex-Mex place and let her try the refried black

beans that came with my meal. I gave her a spoonful and she went totally bonkers over it. I looked away momentarily and her hand reached
across the table at lighting speed and grabbed a handful of beans. She
then smooshed those beans all over her face. She covered her cheeks
with it, and her little, two-tooth grin was massive. We couldn't help but
laugh along with our server and two other tables full of people around
us on the patio. We let her play and eat the beans, tried to use a spoon
that quickly went on the floor, and probably spent ten minutes trying
to clean her up before we left the restaurant. Every time we return, we
talk and smile at the "bean night."

We also tried an inflatable floaty for the bathtub one night that
allowed Harper to float and spin in the bath. We were both watching
her, and she seemed to like it once she was in the warm water. We
Facetimed my parents to show off how cute it all was. About 30 seconds into the Facetime, Harper made a face, and then a massive green
spew of poo came out of her bottom, propelling her forward a few
inches in the tub. My parents, Ryan, and I could not stop laughing.
While it was so gross and required quite a lot of cleanup and extra
washing, it was so funny and will likely be a memory we bring up for
years to come!

Both instances could have been inconvenient and frustrating with
the added work they created. They could have provoked negativity
while we were both sleep deprived. Instead, we embraced the chaos,
accepted we would need more time to clean up, and just ran with it.
We had fun! Going with the flow and being OK with the fact that
things with a baby rarely follow the plan will help you relieve stress and
make the little, messy moments unforgettable.

We also tried to make small milestones memorable as well. While we might not have been able to celebrate holidays, birthdays, and other big moments in the same ways we could pre-baby, we tried to ensure that we still took time to celebrate along the way. For example, on Harper's one-week birthday, we were both exhausted, but we wanted to celebrate that we, as a team, made it through one week of being parents and keeping Harper alive. We also wanted to celebrate her. When we went grocery shopping that day, we bought a birthday cookie, and that night, we put a single candle in the cookie and sang Happy Birthday to Harper. We also taped a candle to her bottle so she could enjoy a fresh, birthday milk after her dad and I helped her blow out the candle. While she had absolutely no idea what was happening, it was an easy way to celebrate everything we had been through as partners and much lover we had for Harper already.

Those little memories add up. In the early months, you are taking on a extraordinarily heavy load. Make sure to recognize all your hard work and give yourself the credit you are due for being a fantastic mom and provider to your baby. If you can, make the time and mental space to celebrate those moments, milestones, and all you have accomplished.

Life with Baby

When you have a baby, you not only bring a new life into this world, but you start a new life for yourself. Your life has changed forever, but that does not mean it is over or bad. Your life is just different. It is different because you will have a plus one with you almost everywhere you go. You can still go places and have experiences, but you will just go at a different pace and have different experiences. Your plus-one walks slower, requires frequent snack breaks, and needs naps, but can still go with you where you want to go. The places you go may change to parks, zoos, libraries, and friends' houses. You will also need to bring way more necessities with you wherever you go (diaper bags, snacks, changes of clothes, strollers, etc.) but you will get the hang of it.

It may feel intimidating to go places or do things with your baby. There can be stress in just figuring out the time you need to leave the house just to get somewhere on time, given nap schedules and feeding times, and packing all the items you need to bring, but you can do it. Don't let anyone tell you otherwise.

You can even travel with a baby. It is possible, but again, it just looks different. Instead of trips that are adventurous or busy, you will need to find places that are family-friendly and build in extra time for breaks and your baby's needs. Traversing airports and planes can seem stressful, but airports and airlines go to great lengths to accommodate families, and people will forgive you or put headphones on if your baby cries on the airplane. Be confident in yourself, do your research, plan extra time for everything you do, and know that you will be okay.

What is the worst thing that can happen, anyways? You forget the diapers?

When Harper was five months old, we took a trip to Fort Lauderdale, Florida, for a long weekend. Everything at the start of our trip, from getting through security to getting onboard the plane, even to take off, went smoothly.

Harper was sitting on my lap about two hours into the three-hour flight when we heard, and I felt, it. A massive poop. We grabbed the diaper bag, pulled out the wipes, and dug, and dug, and dug for diapers. Oh. My. God. There were no diapers in the diaper bag!

I had put an entire sleeve of diapers in the diaper bag but moved them into our checked bag for more carry-on space. The bag with all our diapers was in the belly of the plane. Neither Ryan nor I had checked the diaper bag for additional diapers in the side pockets. We just assumed that diapers were in the diaper bag. Duh.

I took Harper to the restroom and made sure it was not a blowout. It didn't stink thaaaat bad, either. There were no other babies her size on the plane that we could barter a diaper from, so our only option was to wait it out.

Harper was happy as a clam for the remaining hour of the flight. We distracted her with toys, milk, and naps. As soon as we landed and our bags appeared on the baggage claim belt, we grabbed diapers and changed her immediately.

If we can survive the "worst case, no diaper scenario," you can too. If you do get into panic mode before a trip, plan for your worst case. Sometimes, stress-inducing thoughts can live in our minds until we process and plan what we would actually do if those stressful situations occurred. Think through scenarios that makes you panic and figure out how you would address them. Those situations will most likely never occur, but if they do, now you have a plan and can be confident in your ability to overcome them. Once you have your plan, your anxiety will likely dissipate.

Overall, your mindset will play a very large part in your postpartum journey. Make it a priority to look on the bright side. Know that you have a support system and lean on that system to give you strength when you need it. Know that your life, while different, will be incredibly fulfilling and with beautiful memories. Let those little moments of joy add up so that when you look back on these years, you will know you enjoyed every second you could and made the most of your time with your child.

Thoughts from Other Moms:

The mom-friends in my life were my inspiration for this book. I am incredibly lucky to have strong, supportive women around me and my daughter. Those women imparted so many invaluable words of wisdom to me and gave me immeasurable amounts of encouragement in my journey. They wanted to do the same for you. The below notes about postpartum life are addressed to you, with love, from them.

- "All the sayings are true (not that it makes it any easier at the moment). Time is fleeting, this is just a phase, and this too shall pass. You will get through this."

- "The newborn/baby period truly is so fleeting and goes by so fast. The whole saying 'The days are long, but the years are short" is a cliche saying for a reason!'"

- "Know that it's okay not to savor every moment and to wish away the bad days. Not every moment of this first year is fun. It's hard. The hardest thing you will ever do. There are many, many times you will want to or actual-ly will cry and scream out of exhaustion, frustration, you name it."

- "It's not always rewarding at first, but as your newborn gets older and starts responding back to you, your heart will just melt, and those little squeals, smiles, hand squeez-es on your finger—those are the rewards. Seeing your baby grow and develop a personality, that's what makes it all worth it."

- "Someone told me this, and it resonated so much: 'The

days are long, but the years are short.' Just know that the phases in the early days can seem overwhelming, but they will go by so fast; be present, and know you are not alone. You have a tribe of other mothers around you always, and it just keeps getting better and better."

- "You are doing a great job, mom!"

- "If you don't feel like getting out of your PJs before noon, that's ok! You are doing your best! Guilt is easily felt in every aspect of this process but tell that voice to leave immediately."

- "It's not a sprint, it's a marathon. So, take each day as it comes. Don't worry about the next day. And on the really challenging days? Take it one hour at a time. End each day with some reflection and acknowledgement. What sucked…what actually was okay…and what could you do differently next time. Once you realize how much is out of your control and how much is in your control, these things become easier."

- "Celebrate all the wins! There is no such thing as a small victory when you're raising a newborn."

And from the woman who taught me how to be the best mom I can be, my mother:

- "The love you feel for your children lingers in your heart forever. That love and concern for them never leaves you. Breathe, make the best of the situation, and enjoy the ride."

I hope this book has given you comfort and confidence going into the fourth trimester. I wish you and your baby all the love, happiness, and health that this journey can bring. Give yourself grace, nourish your mind, body, and baby, and embrace those around you for support. Remember, you're not alone, you've got this, and you're a good mom. Let your new life as a parent begin!

REFERENCES

American Pregnancy Association. (n.d.). "Postpartum care: Baby Blues." American Pregnancy Association. https://americanpregnancy.org/healthy-pregnancy/first-year-of-life/baby-blues/.

CBS 19 News. (2021). "Being a mom is the equivalent of 2.5 full-time jobs, study shows." https://www.cbs19news.com/story/43461685/being-a-mom-is-the-equivalent-of-25-fulltime-jobs-study-shows#.

Centers for Disease Control and Prevention. (2023, May 22). "Depression Among Women." https://www.cdc.gov/reproductivehealth/depression/index.htm#how

Cleveland Clinic. (2022). Lochia. https://my.clevelandclinic.org/health/symptoms/22485-lochia#:~:text=It%20can%20vary%20between%20people,for%20up%20to%20eight%20weeks.

Cooper, J. A., M.D. (n.d). "Screens and Your Sleep: The Impact of Nighttime Use." Sutter Health. https://www.sutterhealth.org/health/sleep/screens-and-your-sleep-the-impact-of-nighttime-use#:~:text=Studies%20show%20two%20or%20more,other%20type%20of%20relaxing%20activity.

Gianni, M. L., et al. (2019). "Breastfeeding Difficulties and Risk for Early Breastfeeding Cessation." *Nutrients*, 11(10), 2266. https://www.ncbi.nlm.nih.gov/pmc/articles/PMC6835226/.

Iranpour, S., Kheirabadi, G. R., Esmaillzadeh, A., Heidari-Beni, M., & Maracy, M. R. (2016). "Association between sleep quality and postpartum depression." *J Res Med Sci.*, 21, 110. https://www.ncbi.nlm.nih.gov/pmc/articles/PMC5322694/.

Kalaitzandonakes, M., Ellison, B., and Coppess, J. (2023). "Coping with the 2022 infant formula shortage." *Prev Med Rep.*

Mayo Clinic. (2022). "Breast milk storage: Do's and don'ts." https://www.mayoclinic.org/healthy-lifestyle/infant-and-toddler-health/in-depth/breast-milk-storage/art-20046350.

Mayo Clinic. (2022). "Postpartum care: What to expect after a vaginal birth." Mayo Clinic. https://www.mayoclinic.org/healthy-lifestyle/labor-and-delivery/in-depth/postpartum-care/art-20047233.

Mayo Clinic. (2022). "Postpartum Depression." Mayo Clinic. https://www.mayoclinic.org/diseases-conditions/postpartum-depression/diagnosis-treatment/drc-20376623.

Newmark, L., M., (2022). "Baby Backwash Can Trigger Immune Response in Milk." International Milk Genomics Consortium, (110). https://www.milkgenomics.org/?splash=baby-backwash-can-trigger-immune-response-in-milk#:~:text=When%20a%20human%20infant%20suckles,gland%20about%20the%20infant's%20health.

Osborn, C. (2018). "How to Deal with Hemorrhoids After Pregnancy." Healthline. https://www.healthline.com/health/hemorrhoids-after-pregnancy#when-to-see-a-doctor.

Pacheco, D., & Singh, A. (2023). "Exercise and Sleep." Sleep Foundation. https://www.sleepfoundation.org/physical-activity/exercise-and-sleep.

Ruscio, D. (2022). "Resolve Postpartum Insomnia and Get Back to Sleep." https://drruscio.com/postpartum-insomnia/.

Sanford Health. (2023). "The importance of skin-to-skin with baby after delivery." https://news.sanfordhealth.org/childrens/the-importance-of-skin-to-skin-after-delivery-you-should-know/.

Stuebe, A. M., Grewen, K., & Meltzer-Brody, S. (2013). "Association between maternal mood and oxytocin response to breastfeeding." *J Womens Health (Larchmt)*, 22(4), 352-361.

Swanson, L. M., et al. (2020). "Perinatal Insomnia and Mental Health: a Review of Recent Literature." *Current psychiatry reports*, 22(12), p. 73.

U.S. Department of Labor Wage and Hour Division. (2022). "FLSA Protections to Pump at Work." https://www.dol.gov/agencies/whd/pump-at-work#:~:text=The%20Fair%20Labor%20Standards%20Act,need%20to%20express%20the%20milk.

WebMD. (2023). "What Is a Postpartum Belly Wrap?" https://www.webmd.com/baby/what-is-postpartum-belly-wrap#:~:text=Some%20women%20use%20a%20postpartum,place%20after%20having%20a%20baby.

van Veldhuizen-Staas, C. G. A. (2007). "Overabundant milk supply: an alternative way to intervene by full drainage and block feeding." *Int Breastfeed J*, 2(11).

ABOUT THE AUTHOR

Meet Jessica Dawson, a proud, Denver-based mother to her daughter Harper and dog Beans, partner to her husband Ryan, marketing executive, and avid traveler. Inspired by a supportive tribe of remarkable women, she fearlessly penned her first book Postpartum: The Expectations and Reality of the Fourth Trimester to empower new moms with the hard truth of what they may experience with a relatable, fun, and friendly perspective, creating an invaluable resource for everyone embarking on the adventure of motherhood.

For More Postpartum Resources, Visit:
www.PostpartumMomGuide.com